WHOLE

SCHOOL

PROJECTS

WHOLE

SCHOOL

PROJECTS

ENGAGING IMAGINATIONS THROUGH
INTERDISCIPLINARY INQUIRY

KIERAN EGAN

WITH BOB DUNTON & GILLIAN JUDSON

Teachers College, Columbia University
New York and London

Published by Teachers College Press, 1234 Amsterdam Avenue, New York, NY 10027

Copyright © 2014 by Teachers College, Columbia University

Library of Congress Cataloging-in-Publication Data available at www.loc.gov.

ISBN 978-0-8077-5583-9 (paper)
ISBN 978-0-8077-5584-6 (hardcover)
ISBN 978-0-8077-7327-7 (ebook)

Printed on acid-free paper
Manufactured in the United States of America

21 20 19 18 17 16 15 14   8 7 6 5 4 3 2 1

Contents

Acknowledgments

I am most grateful for the numerous exchanges with teachers and administrators involved in current Whole School Projects, particularly David Futter, Jonathan Sclater, Pamela Hagen, Yvan Zebroff, Sheri Dunton, Lindy Sims, and Alyssa Reed-Stuewe. Their work has been inspiring to me and hugely appreciated by their students. In addition, discussions about their Whole School Project work have been really helpful for writing this book. I am also grateful for the comments on the manuscript by Annabella Cant, a PhD student at Simon Fraser University, and also by Elizabeth Branch Dyson of The University of Chicago Press. Their comments enriched the book significantly. I am grateful, too, for permission from The University of Chicago Press to reprint in Chapter 6 of this book some sections from Chapter 5 of my *Learning in Depth: A Simple Innovation that can Transform Schooling*, which was published in 2010. I am also very appreciative for the insightful and most helpful comments of two anonymous reviewers of the manuscript, as you might be as well, because they have stimulated me to make changes that have led to a better organized and more readable text.

I was going to include a note of special thanks to Bob Dunton, principal of Corbett Charter School, and Gillian Judson, lecturer in the Faculty of Education, Simon Fraser University, but their contributions to the manuscript, both in careful reading and rereading, and their own noted contributions within the text, make such an acknowledgment inadequate. And so it seems more appropriate to acknowledge them on the cover. This book would have been significantly diminished without their help.

Introduction

"When God created the universe," a teacher said to me recently, "she didn't divide it into subjects." The universe of knowledge, however, is almost invariably divided into the familiar set of subjects in the curriculum. There have been attempts to introduce children to knowledge of the world and human experience that avoid the usual divisions into subject areas (e.g., Postman & Weingartner, 1969), but none of them has really been entirely satisfactory and none has been sufficiently attractive that they have influenced the curriculum of typical schools. So we still find almost universally in schools the routine differentiation of knowledge into the subjects that are familiar to endless generations of students—math and history, biology and foreign languages, English/language arts and social studies, art and computer studies, and so on. Some divisions have to be made, of course, as one can't simply take on the whole world of knowledge at one go, and the division into the traditional subjects seems also to have suggestive philosophical support, as in Hirst (1974).

The danger many people have pointed to in the subject-divided curriculum is that each subject comes to be seen by students not as a part of a whole, but somehow as distinct bits that never come together in any clear way in their minds. It's the fragmentation of coherence that is seen as a problem of the subject-divided curriculum for many students.

Well, this is perhaps a rather labored way of introducing the purpose of this book. I want to propose a way of addressing this problem, but also a number of others that are produced by our current ways of organizing schools. Inadvertently, and too often unnoticed, aspects of current school organization diminish the educational experience they are designed to provide. Any organization, especially one as vast as our school systems, is bound to involve some compromises between administrative necessity and educational experience. Sometimes, though, the compromises are caused more by administrative convenience than ought to be the case, and when this does happen, a bit of ingenuity might enable us to preserve more of the educational value.

This book will describe a project that can add a lot more to schools' educational value than it costs in administrative inconvenience. Let me briefly sketch an outline of the Whole School Projects I am proposing and then I will look at other benefits and educational values that can result from them.

The idea is that each school will take on a particular topic to study for 3 years. The whole school will be involved in the study. The topic might involve local phenomena—such as "plants and animals of the desert" if the school is in Alamogordo, New Mexico; "sheep farming" if it is in Walworth, New Zealand; "water resources" if it is in West Vancouver, Canada; "the Columbia River Gorge" if it is near Portland, Oregon; "the castle" if it is in Ludlow, England; or "the Yarra River" if it is in Melbourne, Australia; or the natural and cultural environment of three or four blocks around the school if it is in a typical suburban setting. Alternatively, the study could involve quite distant things—such topics as "the solar system," or "desertification and attempts to combat it," "ocean life," "migrating animals," and so on.

All students and all classes will be involved. The rest of the curriculum will continue as it currently is, but some time—maybe no more than 1 or 2 hours each week—will be given during which students and teachers build their knowledge of the chosen topic, directed toward a large-scale final product. While the Whole School Project (WSP) is distinct from, and is in addition to, the regular curriculum, it can help achieve many of the year's curriculum objectives in mathematics, science, art, history, and so on. Any teacher can choose to incorporate his or her curriculum goals into the project study, even when those goals include meeting externally mandated achievement standards.

Ideally the "whole school" referred to is conceived as extending from the beginning of elementary school to the end of high school, though obviously such an ideal will be very rarely achievable. Most schools are elementary schools, middle schools, or high schools. One of the benefits of the Whole School Project comes from students of different ages working together on a common topic. The Whole School Projects will usually be run within an individual elementary, middle, or high school, acknowledging that high school administrators may initially think such projects are too much of a distraction from their tighter curricula constraints and exam schedules.

I will describe the plan in more detail in Chapter 2, after detailing the problems it can help solve in Chapter 1. In Chapter 3, I will step toward the reality of such projects on the ground, as it were, and describe three examples, two of which are currently under way and the third of which is completed. I will largely use the words of teachers involved in them to give an image of how they work in practice. In Chapter 4, I will discuss what kinds of topics serve to provide an adequate Whole School Project for at least 3 years of study, listing a set of criteria that a suitable project will need to meet. Chapter 5 explores a number of practical matters concerned with getting such a project going and keeping students' interest sustained, especially as they might work in class groupings and in cross-age groupings. Chapter 6 looks at learning principles that will ensure the WSP engages students' imaginations in the process. In Chapter 7, I will consider some of the educational principles that support this kind of program and provide a sound educational foundation for it. I will conclude, in Chapter 8, by raising and responding to the main objections that I have heard or imagined may be brought up when implementing WSPs, and try to show that the apparent challenges posed by such projects are really not as daunting as they may initially seem to some people.

Here is a simple list of some of the benefits that I think implementing this kind of Whole School Project can achieve. I will explore these in detail later and suggest others. I will consider the benefits in terms of their potential contributions to the overall community of the school, to teachers, and, most important, to students.

Some benefits for the students:

- Students build an emotional and imaginative engagement in learning about the world and develop pride in the growth of the project.
- Students understand the gradual growth of something very big from many small contributions—"a stone upon a stone, a word upon a word."
- Students are exposed to new interests and to invigorating learning activities they might otherwise not experience.
- Students see how different "subjects" in school overlap and work together when used in a large-scale interdisciplinary project.

Some benefits for the teachers:

- Teachers collaborate in integrated planning and teaching with colleagues.
- Teachers experience a distinctive educational project with distinctive educational activities, in a context of mutual support.

- Teachers build a deeper sense of how distinct disciplinary perspectives can come together in a large-scale interdisciplinary project.

Some benefits for the overall community of the school:

- WSPs contribute powerfully to community building within the school.
- WSPs help students, teachers, and administrators discover how individual contributions to a coherent large-scale project can produce enormous results, helping all participants feel pride for more than just their own individual work.
- WSPs encourage appreciation for the abilities of others, enabling everyone involved to recognize that all kinds of learning styles, intelligence, and ability level can play an important part.

Large-scale projects in schools are hardly new, of course. But nearly all such projects that I am aware of focus on some social or behavioral purpose, such as ecological sustainability, eliminating drugs, prevention of bullying and other "antisocial" behavior, or art projects, health issues, recycling, and other worthy social goals. Also many schools adopt year-long themes of various kinds, which also overlap somewhat with this proposal. Typical themes, however, tend to be focused on some relevant social concern—environmental issues, aboriginal populations, behavioral problems, and so on—and they are very rarely expected to continue for more than a year. The kinds of projects I will propose are designed to contribute to educational purposes that are sometimes not adequately achieved in schools because of how schools are typically organized.

The time and resource costs of implementing such projects may seem daunting, especially to anyone who has never done one. How does one build something on this scale in a school whose organizational and other resources may be already stretched to the limit? I hope that by the end of the book, if you stick with me, it will be clear that the costs of such Whole School Projects need not be great, and the educational benefits to the students' learning and the sense of community for the school as a whole far outweigh any costs. The hard part, as with most things, is beginning. But you've read this far, so let's continue together.

CHAPTER 1

What Is a Whole School Project?

Teachers and students beginning a garden.

In the Introduction, I suggested there is a set of advantages that comes from implementing a Whole School Project. (At the cost of adding yet another acronym to the world, I will call them WSPs for the rest of this book.) Some of the benefits they seem to offer are achieved by school themes and less extensive projects that may not involve the whole school and take a lot less than the 3 years WSPs require. The curriculum has seemed adequate to most people, if not over-adequate, in laying the encyclopedia of human knowledge before children. (*Encyclopedia*—I learned today—comes from the Greek words *enkyklios* and *paideia*, meaning "all-round education.") This is relevant here because WSPs do offer a rare experience of "all-roundness" in exploring a topic. At the same time, there is no shortage of concerns expressed about the adequacy with which we are delivering an "all-round education" to students, so it might be worth exploring whether WSPs might solve some of the problems we face.

One way to consider the problems WSPs can help us solve might be to look at the set of benefits they can bring to students, teachers, and the school and see whether we don't already provide those, in some degree at least, by means of other programs. If I can identify a number of clear educational values that WSPs offer that are not currently provided by other programs, or values that are easily achieved by WSPs that are difficult to achieve with current programs, this would justify introducing WSPs.

I will use the set of benefits to students, teachers, and the school community mentioned in the Introduction, followed in each case by my analysis of whether current programs do or do not adequately deliver each educational value, and why it is a problem if they don't.

Here are the brief headings used earlier, recognizing that these are hardly mutually exclusive categories. Things that benefit the school community will benefit the teachers and students as well. But these categories allow me to focus on the somewhat distinctive benefits to all those who will be involved in the WSP.

Some benefits for students:

Students build an emotional and imaginative engagement in learning about the world and develop pride in the growth of the project.

The selected WSP topic frames some aspect of the world in a way that makes it conceptually manageable. It gives the students a bite-sized chunk to work on, even though it might require quite a big bite and a fair amount of chewing. To take one of the examples described in Chapter 3: The Columbia River Gorge is an enormous geological entity, and it encompasses a huge variety of features, flora and fauna, human activities, settlements, and so on that can be grasped as a whole.

The topic is sorted by first dividing it into sections that different groups can begin to tackle—its geology, geography, plants, animals, insects, transportation patterns, water, history, and so on. Then we see how these parts come together and gradually everyone can see how this massive and diverse topic is nevertheless a comprehensible whole. In coming to comprehend the topic, students will see the value of the various disciplines that build knowledge bit by bit but the focus will constantly be on building an integrated understanding of the topic. While that is always the goal in schools, even with very particular curriculum topics, we are not always successful in achieving it. Too often the drive for disciplinary mastery, and its demonstration in various forms of tests, tends to suppress the task of developing a richer overview that builds more general comprehension. So it does seem that, in this regard at least, WSPs offer a means of achieving an important educational goal that is not commonly achieved in routine schooling today.

There are many schools around the Columbia River Gorge, and most of the students from those schools drive through it or visit parts of it for one purpose or another. But the students for whom the Gorge has been a WSP for 3 years understand its many dimensions in a richly satisfying interdisciplinary and multidisciplinary way, and their sense of it is quite different from that of the students who have not been immersed in learning about it. The knowledge learned by those for whom it has been a WSP is not merely a set of facts, such as a tourist might pick up from a pamphlet about the Gorge, but it is both hugely more extensive and intensive, drawing the students' emotions into the drama of the Gorge's creation and the history that has led to its current range of plants and animals, and into the lives of earlier inhabitants and their struggles. This integrated knowledge also stimulates the wonder that comes with seeing the complexity that has led to what many simply take for granted as some dramatic views and interesting walks: That challenging hike up to the waterfall is enjoyable for most of us but is also, for those students, tied in with their images of the massive torrents that ripped the land apart on its rush to the sea; the history of plant species that followed; why the particular plants, animals, and less visible insects are here now; and where that water is coming from and going to, and so on. The WSP creates a personal connection to the place that engages the imagination. This will not be equally true for all students all the time, but it will be true for many much of the time, and nearly all will get a much richer understanding than most people who live in the area. (And these educational values do not come at the cost of students' performance on standardized tests of various kinds, as will be indicated at the end of the Gorge example in Chapter 3.)

WSPs not only add variety to the forms of learning students engage in, and the contexts in which they learn and what they learn, but they also are excellent tools for engaging the emotions and imaginations of students in learning. Many activities in schools do this, of course, and all activities try to do it. That this kind of engagement is not as routine as we would like is one of the justifications for adding WSPs to the curriculum.

The other feature mentioned, about the pride that develops as the final product is gradually completed, comes both from the achievement itself and the students' recognition of the roles they have played in creating that final product. That pride is also tied up with public appreciation of the display of the project, whether that public is parents, random visitors to the schools, or selected groups to whom the product is presented. The presentation will find a permanent home in the school, but it can also in some form, via some suitable digital medium, be presented in such places as senior homes, to local council members, community centers, or to other groups who might have an interest in the implications of the product. I have been in the school that took on the Gorge, for example, and looked in admiration at the astonishing representation of the Columbia River Gorge along the walls and ceiling of the central corridor, and at the massive amounts of wonderfully displayed information that the students have added to it. And I was aware as I looked in evident delight that students walking by were clearly also delighted at this stranger's appreciation of what they had made and done. This was a kind of individual pride in a large-scale academic achievement that is not common in schools. It is, however, a kind of pride that would be common to students engaged in a WSP; they are proud of how much they know about the topic and proud in its display.

The sense of engagement described here in terms of a single topic around a geological feature in the United States, and the pride of students involved in working toward a final product concerning the topic—in this case a dramatic and complex mural—can be echoed among groups of students anywhere a WSP is under way. You can see the same enthusiasm, for example, in Chinese students in the industrial city of Qingdao, China, as they explore the native flora that has been largely devastated by industrialization, and as they explore how they can make a garden that re-creates within the school an attractive place hospitable to native plants. The students' pride in their accumulating knowledge and also in the gradual growth of their garden mirrors that of any group of students engaged in a WSP. And something similar is the case in Coquitlam, BC, Canada, where students at Westwood Elementary School are remaking their school environment to be symbolically a part of their study of a nearby river. (These are examples we will look at in Chapter 3.) Whether the WSP study is of desertification, the solar system, the above and below ground environment for three blocks around a suburban school, or whatever, and a clear final product for the work is identified, the same imaginative engagement and pride can be evoked in participating students.

These are complex, difficult, and desirable educational benefits that WSPs can deliver routinely.

Students understand the gradual growth of something very big from many small contributions—"a stone upon a stone, a word upon a word."

WSPs deliberately celebrate diversity among students, and recognize the value of many different kinds of contribution by seeing how each student can bring distinctive abilities and skills to a common project. A related goal is that the students see how their individual contributions add to the developing whole.

Sadly, most people never initiate or move forward with a large-scale task and so they do not discover the scale of impact one can have by working consistently on something over a long period. Some people do engage in such a large-scale task and they often feel satisfaction in their achievement—whether building a boat or cabin or house or harpsichord, or buying land and planting an orchard, or refurbishing an old car or airplane, or undertaking a large and difficult journey, or writing a book. They also learn that a concerted and well-planned effort can achieve large-scale results. This is an educational experience that more people might enjoy if they engage in something like it during their school years.

Look at the pyramids, cathedrals, modern skyscrapers, massive-scale food production, railway and airplane transportation systems, road and Internet highways, space exploration projects, and so on. I am not proposing that a school get into the business of interstellar travel or building skyscrapers, but I am proposing that schools ensure that a part of each student's educational experience includes participation in a project that communicates how organized and concerted action by a large number of people can have large effects beyond what they could otherwise have imagined or expected, and also that they comprehend the whole that they are a part of and recognize the tangible contribution to that whole made by their own work.

Cathedrals and complex transportation systems become a little more comprehensible if one engages in a large project cooperating with others. Students who have not experienced anything like WSPs are more likely to simply take these vast achievements for granted, like parts of the natural world, as beyond our making and so not thought of as human constructions that one might set about achieving. The students who have been involved in one or more WSPs will be much more likely to look at the complex world around them in a reflective and analytical way. They will have some experience of putting something very large together with others. It will also make them more likely to take on such tasks themselves, simply because they have a sense that large-scale achievements are possible. They will recognize their own contributions as cogs in machines, but they will also understand that even the most complex machines and systems can be made and remade, and that cogs are vital; they need not be unconscious of the importance of their roles.

Students are exposed to new interests and to invigorating learning activities they might otherwise not experience.

The latter part of this claim can be recognized as true simply on formal grounds. The way students commonly learn while engaged in a WSP involves a variety of contexts that will likely be quite new in their experience of schooling. Once the project is divided up for attention by the different classes and groups involved, individual students might find themselves sometimes working with their whole class, sometimes with a group within their class, and sometimes with groups that involve older and/or younger students from different classes. The groups and their deployment will be decided by the general purpose built into the project and also by the smaller-scale structuring of the studies organized by the committee that will be running the WSP. Groups of students will be given specific tasks as the project goes forward.

It has been consistently shown in a number of studies that students learn best when they are actively involved in either formal or informal learning groups or study teams (Barkley, Cross, & Major, 2005; Davis, 1993; Michaelsen, Knight, & Fink, 2002). A number of these studies suggest that students learn more of what is taught and retain this information longer than when the same content is presented in other instructional formats. Students who work in collaborative groups also appear more satisfied with their learning experience. If properly organized, these groups help students develop a number of skills that add to their abilities to organize their work, delegate tasks among the group, and become more effective at communicating and cooperating. The key phrase there is "if properly organized;" none of this happens by magic simply by putting students into groups. The WSP also involves helping students learn the skills that will make them more effective learners within groups. There are many books, articles, and Internet sources that can guide the organizers of WSPs in how to make group learning most effective. All students do not take to such group learning with equal enthusiasm or ease, but class groups and the others that will be formed during the project can be made very effective learning environments, and they will offer some variety to students' learning beyond what is commonly available in everyday classrooms.

The first part of the claim above suggests that WSPs will routinely expose students to new interests. Often one sees in educational writing the claim that one should always begin a new study from what students are already interested in. This makes some sense and can be an effective tool in attracting students' interest to something new by showing its connection to something that they are already interested in. But one of the purposes of education is to develop new interests for students, and sometimes the most educationally valuable come from discovering new areas of knowledge. Commonly it is recognized that novelty and variety stimulate imaginations and interest. I'm not sure that novelty and variety are always the best principles to build with, however, as they can easily lead to a "touristic" approach to education if overused. The purpose for WSPs is to develop an enriched appreciation of areas of knowledge that might be quite new to students, or, if not new—as in the case of three blocks around the school or some local natural or cultural feature—then not so taken-for-granted that the intense focus the WSP provides opens up dimensions of the topic that make it new for the students.

So the intensity of understanding that the WSP is designed to build, for most students, constitutes something new in their schooling experience. Working with the whole school on the same topic should also have a multiplier effect on students developing new interests in the topic of the WSP as they learn. One thing about interest is that it is somewhat contagious—maybe not quite as contagious as enthusiasm for a new song or sporting event—but it is ahead of most things that flicker into our notice during the day, and even ahead of colds and flu! The contagious enthusiasm for accumulating knowledge and building toward the planned final product of a WSP is actually pretty high on the contagion scale in the implementations of such projects so far.

If the WSP is adequately designed, there will be a continuing sense of progress toward the final product, and a sense of progress in a project is also a significant contributor to holding and intensifying interest. Though one doesn't necessarily want to play with this too much, the sense of suspense created by whether or not the final product will be completed in time can also be a significant stimulator of interest in the final year of work. And although I suggested novelty can be overdone very easily as an educational principle, it is also obvious that some

unexpected findings, or some aspect of the WSP that no one had anticipated, can be a significant deepener and extender of students' interest
in the topic. This can't be planned for, but some greater or small novelty
will occur in all WSPs, and the organizing committee should be aware of
their best deployment for enriching interest.

Also, the kind of expertise available in the community that can be
attracted to a large-scale project with potential public ramifications is
much greater than can be attracted by a single teacher dealing with
a specific topic. University professors are expected to do "community
service" as a part of their work, and so WSP planners can begin to think
about how the range of expertise available in a local college or university
can add to the dimensions of their topic. There will also be public officials and engineers available who will be happy to speak to students. It's
not that some of these experts would not be invited to address students
in the normal course of a school's activities, but that the WSP legitimizes
the invitation of experts who can interact with the students on the topic,
about which the students will already have considerable knowledge to
further motivate the interest and enthusiasm of the visiting expert. Such
specialists can also address many classes at one time; economies of scale
would come into play with WSPs.

Good teaching will always open students up to new interests. What
WSPs do offer, in addition to interest, is exposure to a wider range of
potential interests as a result of engaging with the various dimensions
of the project. Perhaps it might be a fascination for insect life, begun
from tracking certain insects' movements around the site of the project,
or rock formations, or graphic comics as a result of constructing one on
the movements and adventures of deer around the hilltop school site, or
fossils as a result of discoveries on the project site, or birds from tracking
with binoculars the kinds of birds that live on or cross over the site, and
any of these can lead to students' beginning collections of rocks, bird
feathers, leaves, seeds, and so on.

**Students see how different "subjects" in school overlap and work
together when used in a large-scale interdisciplinary project.**

I began with the quotation from a teacher who suggested that the
universe was not divided into subjects. The fact that schoolwork usually is split this way can create some confusion for students. School
subject divisions are a product of how we have learned to explore and
study the world, and it makes sense to follow the kinds of inquiries that
have been most productive for us. While we accumulate knowledge

and methodological skill in learning mathematics and science, history, and the arts, while in the process dealing with math problems, science experiments, history questions, and artistic creations, many of the questions we deal with in life do not present themselves in disciplinary terms. We respond to many of the issues of our lives by applying our disciplinary-gained knowledge and skills in interdisciplinary contexts. So, in dealing with a question raised by the city council to introduce more bike lanes, one needs to bring to mind mathematical knowledge to assess the numbers of cars and buses and also cyclists, one needs to bring economic and social considerations to mind on the impact on shop owners, gradient issues might call on physics, effects of climate will draw on geography, making one's arguments will draw on language arts, and so on. It has also been argued that participating in interdisciplinary activities enables students to understand more clearly the value of what they are learning, and so they are likely to become more actively engaged (Resnick, 1989). Also, applying knowledge learned in disciplinary areas to problems beyond those areas stimulates greater flexibility in understanding of the knowledge they have learned and leads to greater transfer of that knowledge to new areas (Collins, Brown, & Newman, 1989).

Again, projects and other activities in schools can help overcome the restriction to understanding that can result from always studying the world in terms of academic subjects. The usual context of classrooms and students' everyday experience of the curriculum tend to reinforce rigidity in applying knowledge to problems different from those in terms of which one learned it. One of the more shocking findings of recent decades comes from the study of Harvard physics students when faced with problems based on knowledge they had learned but set in unfamiliar contexts. Typically these students gave answers that were confused and much the same as those of typical 4-year-olds (see an interesting discussion of this in Gardner, 1993, Chapter 1). Attempts to overcome this general problem of the potential dangers of inflexibility are sporadic in the regular classroom, though the problem becomes keener as students move through the years of schooling. WSPs are designed to teach disciplinary knowledge that is then applied in interdisciplinary settings. Again, while the WSP does not offer a unique method of addressing this educational problem, it does offer a new and potent one. We are not currently being sufficiently successful that we do not need to consider the potent help WSPs offer in addressing what is, after all, a significant educational problem.

Some benefits for teachers:

Teachers collaborate in integrated planning and teaching with colleagues.

One can too readily perceive teachers as leading somewhat isolated professional lives. But they do normally work out of sight and sound of one another for the most part, and most commonly they plan their teaching alone, and have to deal with the daily problems with individual students, parents, and the curriculum alone. There is a continuum from schools in which this image of isolated teachers is the actual daily experience to schools in which there is among teachers a high degree of communication, joint planning, collaboration in preparing materials and gathering resources, co-teaching, and active discussion about educational issues. There are no prizes for working out which end of the continuum aligns with low-performing schools and which with high-performing schools.

There are many books and articles that show the benefits of teacher collaboration and its impact on improved learning and improved job satisfaction for teachers (e.g., Goddard, Goddard, & Tschannen-Moran, 2007; McClure, 2008; Thousand, Villa, & Nevin, 2006). The array of documented benefits include better retention of new teachers and increased satisfaction of new teachers, which also leads to reduced turnover rates, increased student performance in mathematics and reading achievement, and an improved sense of community within the school.

One common finding from studies of schools' use of collaboration among teachers is that simply recommending it does little. There must be support structures in place, scheduled time for teachers' planning meetings, and some defined purpose. WSPs provide a context in which cooperative planning and teaching become routine. Also, organization of a WSP requires the administration to put in place the material and other support whose absence in many schools has undermined hopes for the improvements collaborative work can provide. As with any innovation, it won't work simply by willing it into existence or recommending it. What is also needed are structures, commitment, and effort. The WSP offers a context in which these aspects can maximize the benefits of collaborative work among teachers for enriching the community of the school in general, and ensuring the benefits to teachers of a workplace in which collaborative work is routine and effective. That effectiveness follows from teachers being able to gain from one another's strengths and also support one another's weaknesses. Working in groups they can reduce the amount of time each individually spends planning, and their mutual contributions greatly increase the ideas and materials that are produced.

These benefits are possible in schools without the use of a WSP, but they are rare and harder to achieve. The WSP creates conditions for collaboration. It is also the case, informally observed so far, that schools that take on a WSP find that the collaborative work of teachers does not remain confined to the WSP but begins to involve other work and teaching practice. The WSPs support a culture of cooperative planning and co-teaching in schools.

Teachers experience a distinctive educational project with distinctive educational activities, in a context of mutual support.

One of the benefits WSPs offer to teachers is a somewhat unusual kind of educational experience. Many teachers do become involved in extended projects, which might run for a month or a semester or even a year, and they may become involved in cooperative planning and co-teaching with colleagues. I am unaware of any reliable statistics about how common such projects are. The smaller-scale projects no doubt are more common, if only because of the problems of organizing larger-scale projects. WSPs are distinct in a number of ways from other forms of the project, not only because of their extent and their requirement for a public product at their conclusion, but more importantly because they offer a distinctive kind of teaching experience.

There is no need to elaborate this distinctive experience for teachers here, as the rest of the book will be providing just such an elaboration. The following section on the benefits of WSPs to the whole school community will expand on ways in which teachers' work in WSPs will be unlike nearly all their other experience of teaching and learning in schools. But it is worth emphasizing that one of the significant benefits of the WSP is that it engages teachers in new ways and involves them in new kinds of teaching within a context that is constantly supportive. In large part this is brought about by the commitment that setting up a WSP requires from the administration of the school and the whole school community. This is connected to the reasons many schools might think taking on a WSP is too much. The commitment is to gradually build knowledge and skills about some specific topic in a large-scale collaborative way, organized by a committee (discussed later) that will be alert to how the whole is proceeding. The scale of the WSP will create conditions and involvement unlike nearly all other teaching formats. I am tempted to say, while being wary of the associations, that a WSP is more like organizing an army to take a particular objective than like the usual routines of teaching. The struggles to finally pull everything together to attain the final objective of the WSP can stimulate something more like enthusiastic camaraderie among teachers and students than the more anemic term *collaboration* suggests.

Teachers build a deeper sense of how distinct disciplinary perspectives can come together in a large-scale interdisciplinary project.

Students' experience of the world, when seen through a curriculum that is divided into traditional disciplines, creates a potential problem for them that is mirrored also in the effects such disciplinary divisions have on teachers. Some of these I have mentioned above when discussing the ways WSP can help overcome the potential problems of a discipline-directed focus on the world for students. Teachers are generally trained to specialize in some distinct subject area, even though they might find themselves teaching other subjects day to day. Whatever attempts are made to develop interdisciplinary methods of teaching and structuring the curriculum, it is hard to eliminate the fragmentation of knowledge that our disciplinary understanding of the world has created for us, even though it is clear that interdisciplinary teaching can deliver very significant benefits (Bolak, Bialach, & Duhnphy, 2005; Flowers, Mertens, & Mulhall, 1999).

One prominent way of bringing out the connections and wholeness of the world is to focus on a topic that has some complexity, which is what WSPs aim to do. I will later discuss the criteria for choosing a good topic, but among them is this sense of richness and complexity in which the goal of the exploration, and the final product aimed for, is what determines how the exploration comes together. Although some teachers might focus on the mathematics connected with the project, the ways in which the WSP requires constant collaboration and calibration with others and their inquiries ensures that it is the topic and not the discipline that is in the driving seat. This is not an argument in favor of reducing disciplinary work, of course, but rather making the point that teachers' experience of working within a WSP will inevitably require their constantly seeing how their contributions have to be seen in an interdisciplinary perspective, which they also need to make clear to students as it becomes clear to themselves. This collaboration and calibration adds freshness to teaching and also adds to teachers' learning of the contributions made by other disciplines to their growing knowledge and understanding of the topic. Although there are other ways teachers can sometimes bring such interdisciplinary perspectives to their daily work, it is much easier, and quite routine, in a WSP.

Some benefits for the overall community of the school:

WSPs contribute powerfully to community building within the school.

Traditionally many schools used to require students to wear uniforms, as private or independent schools and some other schools do today. By setting oneself apart from others, one establishes a sense of identity, marked very obviously in one's clothing. Even schools that do not wear daily uniforms do have team-sport uniforms and badges or logos of some kind. These are just outward signs of a sense of community that schools usually try to foster, sometimes well and often in a rather lackadaisical way. Some people—some students, teachers, and administrators—love the ethos that can be created by such means, but for others, of course, the rah-rah enthusiasm of schools that are always insistently emphasizing their sense of difference and, usually, superiority is seen as a pain, and something they want no part of. Yet, when achieved well, there is obviously something of educational value in being a part of a defined learning community and identifying with its values.

Traditional schools commonly divided up the students into smaller groups within the overall community. There might be four to six "houses" that students would be assigned to, and the house would also work to develop house loyalty and encourage students to strive to win "house points" through various team-sport efforts, academic achievements, or volunteer activities. More modern schools often form "families" and "teams" to achieve much the same results. Teachers, too, would be assigned to "houses," "families," or teams, leading regular meetings to encourage "team spirit" or "house loyalty."

A distinctive sense of community means that children who share in it feel comfortable and secure in their school environment, and that leads to more effective learning. Community builds trust in and tolerance of the diversity of members of the community. Fisher (1995) likens a sense of community in a school to a good orchestra working together, even though the players often have different instruments and different roles; they are all contributing to a common end in whose achievement they all share. In such a condition students tend to be more caring of one another, they cooperate more readily, and they support one another's learning. Done properly, such community construction does not encourage students to become complacent drones settling into an environment created and sustained by others, but each student recognizes that he or she has a responsibility to play an active role in sustaining and contributing to the community.

Teachers and administrators are essential for giving the lead to such a sense of community. As Fisher (1995) puts it: "The children look to us to set the tone for caring and learning, and they copy what we do. If we listen to them, they listen to each other. If we value them and support, encourage, and celebrate what they do, they will do the same for each other. If we encourage risk taking and accept approximations, they do the same for themselves and for others. If we are learners in the classroom, they become learners, too" (p. 3). Commonly, schools that build such a sense of community also explicitly make clear, through the various forms of literature the school produces and on its website and in its verbal interactions with students and visitors, that a central value of the school is the creation and preservation of a professional learning community. They also display it in their daily behavior, such that the teacher might greet each child with a handshake, and consistently use the language of "respect for one another" or "listen carefully to what X is saying." Each school can develop its own rituals to reinforce the sense of community in ways that will make it a genuine and welcoming community.

There have been many books about how to organize schools as caring communities, the best of which involve theoretical profundity and practical wisdom (notably Noddings, 2005, among many of her important works). So we have no shortage of good advice and models to follow. And yet this work goes hand in hand with what seems an inexorable decline in the sense of community in society at large and in schools as well (Putnam, 2000, 2002). The best schools today are as good as communities, and perhaps better than in the past, but the worst schools are pretty catastrophic as communities, and the large middle range seems to be sagging downward.

The problem with the models and the excellent published guides about how to make one's school a better community is that to achieve these exemplary ideals requires superior people, outstanding commitment and dedication, and virtuoso teachers and administrators (Sergiovanni, 1994). When I have visited such schools—and there are many of them—I come away awed by the energy and dedication of the fantastic people who are working in them. And this is the problem for so many descriptions of how to improve our schools—they require heroic qualities that are, by definition, rare. It is not to take anything away from the teachers who staff our schools to note that theirs is a job, not a total life commitment to heroic activity. They usually do that job with more commitment than most people working today in factories or banks or shops, but they cannot day in/day out show the kind of heroic commitment that the most outstanding teachers do.

Ordinary teachers and administrators, however, *can* run WSPs. The WSP program represents a technique; and the value of techniques is that they enable us to do routinely what otherwise requires heroic individual commitment. With a well-designed technique we can do what otherwise calls on greater virtue or ingenuity or effort than most of us can manage in the daily grind. I will try to show how a well-designed WSP can achieve for a regular school the community values recommended in the literature that promotes community values in schools.

WSPs are designed to produce something from the work of teachers and students that is beyond the experience of nearly all schools currently. The scale of the product is crucial here, as are the social or cultural uses. While beginning to explore the possibilities for such projects here, it is certain that I am unable to imagine some of the products that schools that take on a WSP will come up with. Many of my suggestions will simply be extensions and expansions from the kinds of projects one can see in schools today, especially in some of the larger-scale projects (Katz & Chard, 2000) and in Place-based environmental schools (Judson, 2010). I will mainly mention studies of geological features, local environments, space, and so on, though I will push beyond these limits when discussing possible topics in Chapter 4.

Another difference between WSPs and the kinds of themes that are common in schools today—such as a focus on reducing bullying, on ecological sustainability, or on eliminating drugs—concerns the deliberate intellectual, academic, cultural focus, as well as concluding with a publicly accessible product.

So WSPs can offer something on a larger scale than schools usually produce, the products can provide an unusual range of educational values, and they have public utility beyond what schools typically manage today. One sees some projects that work in this direction, but nothing that offers the richness and range of educational experiences in creating such a product. Here again, WSPs offer educational benefits that are currently available to relatively few students.

WSPs help students, teachers, and administrators discover how individual contributions to a coherent large-scale project can produce enormous results, helping all participants feel pride for more than just their own individual work.

The overt goal for normal classroom activities is that each student learns the content of the curriculum being taught. The focus is on each student's mastery of math or science or historical material. The normal experience of students in schools is not cooperating on the construction of some jointly understood activity. If the whole class is learning about fractions, they are not cooperating to do anything with that knowledge: It is an individual attainment, and they will individually be tested on how well they have learned it.

Schooling itself is a vast enterprise and we recognize we have a role in this system, but our consciousness of our own actions is rarely recognized in a vivid way as contributing daily to the general enterprise. Rather, we focus on that particular set of students we will meet, our objectives for the next few lessons, the relationships with our colleagues, or some new program we are inclined to try. Our professional teaching association and its issues occasionally may introduce us to our work in larger contexts. But the sheer scale and complexity of the school system is such that it is hard to feel that one's individual contribution has an observable impact on the whole. There is a tendency to see the whole as too vast for one really to comprehend it.

But are schools currently failing to offer students the experience of contributing to something on a large scale of which they can feel a valued part? Well, certainly projects of many kinds are common in schools, and these require understanding an end goal, collaboration and coordination with others in the process of attaining that goal, and satisfaction in achieving something larger than the individual student could manage alone. The Project Approach, as developed by Lilian Katz and Sylvia Chard (2000; projectapproach.org), is widely used and provides children with the experience of in-depth and active exploration of some real-world topics in collaboration with others. It seems fair to say that Katz and Chard have taken what was a somewhat technical pedagogical tool and expanded it into a philosophy of teaching and learning.

The Project Approach is largely derived from William H. Kilpatrick's (1918) attempt to invigorate learning by adapting John Dewey's ideas into a practical technique in which children were to acquire experience and knowledge by solving practical problems in social situations. But Kilpatrick in turn was drawing on older European ideas:

> The "project" is a concept dating from the 17th and 18th centuries, belonging in the same category as the "experiment" of the natural scientist, the "case study" of the jurist, and the "sand-table exercise" of the staff officer. It was introduced

in the curriculum so that students could learn at school to work independently and combine theory with practice. (Knoll, 1997, p. 79)

So if projects, and themes, of various kinds are already available to give students a sense of participating in a group with a coordinated practical purpose, what need do we have of WSPs, and, anyway, how are these different from what has clearly been around for at least 100 years in schools? WSPs seem not to be the solution to a problem in this case because we don't have an absence of practices that give students the experience of contributing to a large whole.

Clearly WSPs are not some entirely distinctive new program, and they clearly borrow some features from the Project Approach and other techniques for gathering students into groups to learn about their world in active ways. But they are different, in relation to this issue, in that they are organized in such a way that the overall project is on a larger scale than is common for school projects, it has a deliberate and significant goal and product, it involves serious academic content, and it deliberately and consistently exposes students to how the whole is developing and provides means for their individual contributions to be seen as important to that developing whole. One of the specific organizational principles of WSPs is to make evident the gradual attainment of a large result from the coordinated contributions of the whole school.

Most students do not have the experience of large coordinated project work at all. Many experience smaller-scale projects, perhaps in a single class and perhaps for a short term. I have seen hardly any reference to projects that are designed to go beyond a year, and few that involve the whole school. The problem to which the WSP concept is offered as a solution is this general absence of the kind of educational experience that WSPs offer, which is barely available to students. There are, unquestionably, projects that offer some aspect of what WSPs are designed to achieve, but they are relatively rare and, at their best, provide only a taste of the educational banquet WSPs can deliver.

WSPs encourage appreciation for the abilities of others, enabling everyone involved to recognize that all kinds of learning styles, intelligence, and ability level can play an important part in constructing the whole.

In schools today learning is constantly assessed. Results of the assessments powerfully influence students' life chances and job prospects. We can forget or fail to notice how deeply this culture of assessment shapes the environment of the school and those who work in it. It comes as a shock to discover that nearly all 7-year-olds when asked why they are in school reply, "To get a job" (Cullingford, 1991). This is not an environment designed to build an appreciation of the abilities of other students and have other students appreciate one's own. (Mind you, the "to get a job" response may not mean as much as might be too quickly inferred. Maybe the children give this response, not because they believe it, but because they have no better understanding of why they are in school that they can articulate as easily, or maybe they think that is the answer the questioner is looking for.)

Good teachers constantly try to undercut the coercive message being delivered by those who require the assessments, but the message is built into the fabric of the institution, and it takes heroic energy and wisdom for teachers to work out how to overcome its pervasive influence on the consciousness of students. By definition, most teachers and administrators cannot bring heroic energy and wisdom to the task, which is why those 7-year-olds unresistingly imbibe the message of the system that assesses them so regularly and delivers rewards and punishments in proportion to achievements on the tests. Even so, in the everyday environment of a good school and nurturing classroom, students can indeed learn to appreciate the abilities of others. Teachers who encourage negotiating, sharing, and compromise in the daily interchanges among students will certainly help build appreciation for the abilities of others, and this is a standard subject in teacher education programs, whether or not it is effectively taught or demonstrated.

So this particular educational value is not that uncommon in regular schools. However, it is a value that WSPs can bring out much more vividly and powerfully than is usually the case in regular school programs and curriculum activities, as I will show in the next chapter.

As students move from class to class in the average school, each teacher calls on the same set of intellectual skills in much the same way. There are variations, of course, and some teaching styles engage some different learning styles among the students. But by and large, each student's daily experience involves attending to teachers' discussion of facts and concepts; reading about them in texts, whether on paper or online; answering some comprehension questions; doing some exercises that test whether the facts and concepts have been learned and understood; engaging in some hands-on experiments; working in groups; and so on. While there is *some* variety in each day, the basic diet provided by the average school is not too varied day in and day out, year in and year out (Goodlad, 2004; Jackson, 1990; Lortie, 2002).

Educational thinkers and reformers have made consistent efforts to change the relatively unvarying experiences of the typical classroom. We have benefitted from Comenius's 17th-century methodological innovations (Murphy, 1995), Pestalozzi's 18th-century ideas (Gutek, 1978), Herbert Spencer's 19th-century evolution-inspired practices (Egan, 2002), and the flood of ideas that constitute the Progressivist movement that continues today, evident recently in the creative work of Howard Gardner (1983, 2006, 2009). In addition, nearly all educational publishers count among their best-selling books for teachers those that describe strategies for dealing with students of mixed ability level (e.g., Tomlinson, 2004). Earlier, I also mentioned the Project Approach and its way of diversifying classroom routines.

The domination of Progressive ideas in teacher education programs, and the pervasiveness of knowledge about and attention to learning styles, multiple intelligences, and ability levels would make it seem that students today should not lack programs and pedagogies that are sensitive to such things. No teacher can be unaware of the ideas about diversity among learners and how to deal with that diversity and even use it for the general enrichment of all students' learning. So what can WSPs add that is not already commonplace in educational practice? To what problem related to recognizing student diversity can WSPs be seen as an answer?

First, it must be recognized that the impossibility of being sensitive to all the varied capacities and diversity of students in a classroom inevitably means some homogenization of treatment. Even with the fullest knowledge of students' diversity and the most energetic attempt to teach in ways that honor those differences, no teacher can hope to adequately attend to them all or even a fraction of them. Even the most brilliant teachers can hope to implement only a portion of the recommended practices available. In fact, there is an awful sense that the more researchers indicate differences among learners, the harder they make it for the conscientious teacher to manage in a typical classroom. A number of years ago, for example, researchers suggested that we should identify differing aptitudes for learning in different students, and then develop appropriate "treatments"—methods of teaching—suitable for students with particular aptitudes (Cronbach & Snow, 1977). When only a few aptitudes had been identified—for example, between "serialist" and "holist" learners (Pask, 1976)—teachers might indeed be made aware that some of their students would be serialists and some holists, and so they could devise strategies to better engage the two kinds of learners. But once researchers had identified six, then a dozen, then 20 different aptitudes, it was not clear what the teacher was to do. In addition, teachers were supposed to accommodate their teaching to various accounts of students' developmental stages, from Herbert Spencer's evolutionary model, with its implications for teaching spelled out in the 1850s and still influential today, and then, of course, Piaget's model, and also that of Erikson, and Kohlberg's model of moral development, and then all the characterizations of differences in terms of intelligence and kinds of intelligence. It can make the head spin. In the end, the sensible teacher seems to use her or his native common sense in attending to the different students in any class. It is not clear that all the information from all these researchers can in practice offer more to teachers than applying their common sense. I know—that's heresy, especially in a "scientific," "evidence-based" environment, but what other conclusion can be reached when intricate theories bump up against common sense? The danger of these schemes individually is that they highlight some differences among students but, in doing so, they suppress attention to others. The danger of them en masse is that they overwhelm the teacher with too much information. Their benefit, it must also be noted, is that they alert those teachers who need such alerting that they should try to accommodate their style of teaching to suit some of the variety in modes of learning among their students.

The structure of the regular classroom creates significant uniformity in the way students are taught and learn. WSPs can be designed to enlist a much wider range of abilities, learning styles, and learning contexts over the 3 years of their existence. A significant amount of the work may be done outside the school, and even when back in the classroom, much of the work will be unlike that for regular classes. I'll explore all this in some detail in later chapters, but here it is sufficient to note that WSPs do offer educationally valuable and diverse forms of learning and teaching that are commonly much more constrained in regular classrooms. It is an explicit goal of WSPs to ensure that individual differences be accommodated in the organization of the project. One can hardly do this limitlessly, but it will be an explicit part of planning to provide a range of educationally valuable experiences that are currently very rare or nonexistent in regular classrooms.

Principals usually spend time and energy trying to promote pride in the school. Too often, perhaps, the object of the sense of pride is the football, basketball, or other sports team, involving the cheerleaders, uniforms, school colors, and so on. In schools with a keen focus on academic achievement, the number of students going on to top-ranked universities is projected as an appropriate source of pride for the school. The trouble with these examples as the main objects of pride in a school is that they work best for the few who are centrally involved in them—the players, cheerleaders, academically outstanding students, and so on. They also encourage some pride in the less active students who are there to cheer or engage in other support activities. But that leaves significant numbers who find the whole team business alienating and a bit pathetic, or who do not anticipate becoming academic high-fliers or even enjoy much academic success at all. (The other slightly odd feature of the default position of pride devolving to the school football team is that football is hardly the point of school.) There does seem to be a problem that WSPs can contribute toward solving.

WSPs can generate pride in being a participant in a large-scale and valued project that is concerned with what schools are supposed to be centrally about—education—and they can engage the commitment of all students, not just the gifted few, while condemning the rest to either more or less enthusiastic fandom or alienation. This general engagement of commitment isn't going to happen automatically, and careful planning has to go into both the choice of the topic for the project and also how each class and each student is given valued and engaging work to do as part of the project. But, if WSPs can get those right, it seems clear that they can provide an educationally valuable experience in which students not only feel pride for their particular contribution in the overall process but also feel pride in the final large product and in everyone else's contributions to it.

I will add that I am not recommending WSPs replacing the football team! The school teams, cheerleaders, clubs, and leadership groups should go on as usual making their contributions to school life, but I am suggesting that WSPs can offer an alternative source of pride in the school, one that is closely aligned with its central educational functions, and one that is more inclusive of the school population as a whole.

Not all schools are made up of very diverse populations, of course, but many are, and all have some diversity. One goal of schooling in a democracy is to ensure that all students have opportunities for equitable participation in school activities and that everyone's contributions are appreciated. Also, educators are increasingly aware of how race, culture and ethnicity, gender, sexual orientation, and physical and mental ability—all of which are fundamental to a student's sense of identity—influence access to education and educational attainments.

Do WSPs offer some new kind of cooperation among diverse student populations? Probably not. Most schools work hard to accommodate diversity and there are a range of programs developed to honor diversity and encourage cooperation. What WSPs can offer is a program that is not overtly concerned with recognizing students' diversity while at the same time encouraging cooperation among students in all groups, ages, and ability levels in producing something with which they can identify and also take pride in. Jointly producing something that all contribute to, and which each student can feel is theirs and their joint achievement, can be a potent contribution to the development of mutual respect and understanding.

Having put it rather negatively, one could easily imagine ways in which diversity among students can be used to enrich the WSP. If, for example, a river is part of the topic being studied, aboriginal students could lead research into the symbolic meanings the river has had in their traditions, immigrant students from Europe might compare it with rivers near their past homes, Hindu students from India might contribute information from their cultures about beliefs in the magical powers of rivers like the Ganges and see whether there are any settlers' accounts with related characteristics, South American students might add a segment on their cultures' myths about river fish and search out local folklore about fish in the river studied in the WSP, and Muslim and Jewish students might explore ideas about rivers in paradise in their traditions and relate these ideas to the topic, and so on.

So WSPs do not offer a unique contribution to diverse student populations, but they can contribute a distinctive support to schools' general aims with regard to diversity, and, with a little ingenuity, can become potent tools in supporting cooperation among different groups.

* * *

Teaching is tough. Schools are complex and often somewhat embattled institutions with multiple stakeholders making competing demands. In the world of schooling, it is hardly any wonder that we can identify a number of educational goods that are currently not ideally well delivered, and some that get only sparse attention. WSPs are not being recommended as some wonderful panacea that can't go wrong and will solve all our problems. What they can do, however, is add a component to most schools' curricula and instructional methods that can contribute a number of important educational goods. Nothing so valuable comes free, of course, and the main cost here is going to be an administrative and organizational one. The promise that WSPs can solve the problems described in this chapter sounds good, no doubt, but the reader will want to know what it would take to get such a project up and running in a typical school. I will next present some examples of WSPs already up and running, then explore the principles and detailed practices that make them work best.

In conclusion, the normal schooling experience for most students, teachers, and administrators does not provide to satisfactory degree a number of the educational goods described above. These inadequacies constitute the problem. Some schools and some teachers in some contexts do respond more than adequately to one or another of these problems, but there is no regular feature of the curriculum—a technique—designed to attack these inadequacies directly and consistently. That is where WSPs will contribute to a solution to these not trivial educational shortcomings of typical schools.

CHAPTER 2

Creating Whole School Projects

Students, soil, and seeds get together.

By laying out some of the problems to which WSPs offer a solution, I have introduced my proposal. I should add at this point that the proposal is for these large-scale projects to become a regular feature of schools' operations. Currently some schools use projects of various kinds, some, very rarely, even extending beyond a single year, but these are typically seen as exotic activities to be admired but certainly not to be taken on by many or all schools. This proposal argues that the educational value of WSPs is such that it doesn't make sense to restrict them to just a few schools with enterprising and energetic principals. They should be designed so that any school can take them on without heroic exertions. The goal of this book is to show how such major projects can be made to work without large support and funding, but as a part of a school's normal educational activity. I will return to this point when making the foundational arguments for WSPs in the final chapter, but I want to make the point early that this proposal is for an innovation that is intended for widespread implementation.

The WSP is never intended to absorb the whole curriculum—it may need saying, though I take that for granted. That is, a WSP is a supplement to the curriculum, not a replacement for anything currently in place. It will certainly be the case that, in planning the project, account will need to be taken of the mandated skills and knowledge that can be best achieved within the project, and it can serve, in that sense, as another component of the school's activities that will contribute to state-mandated skills and knowledge and attaining common core standards. But the school curriculum as it is currently structured and taught will continue much as it is. The WSP might involve a class or two a week, and perhaps a fieldtrip or two each semester; any teacher can use her or his ingenuity in combining aspects of the regular curriculum with the WSP.

DURATION OF WHOLE SCHOOL PROJECTS

Three years seems an optimal time to be able to take on and complete a large-scale exploration of the kinds of topics I will suggest for these projects. Less time doesn't usually allow students to master the depth and diversity of the topic, and more time becomes increasingly administratively inconvenient, with the added danger that the topic might become stale and routine. So the project would normally begin in September of year 1 and conclude in June 3 years later.

At the conclusion of the project in the 3rd year there should be a gap year before another project is begun. That gap year would be used both to celebrate the previous topic and its finished form and to plan for the next. The celebration would involve presentations to parents and civic bodies, to community groups, to injecting the project into relevant political discussions, and more simply to enjoy it and take pride in the finished achievement. Alternative presentations can also be worked on— if the product is in the form of a mural or book or some other form of physical display, it can be adapted for Internet presentation if this hasn't already been done during the making of the project itself. Or the various records, such as videos, which might not have been previously incorporated into the final product, can be worked in during this year, perhaps creating a documentary of the whole WSP process. So the gap year can be seen as a time for also polishing or augmenting or publishing the final form of the project. Also, it will be the time when each child and teacher who has been involved will receive some record of the achievement for themselves—such as a DVD or book, for example.

Proposing a 3-year span for these projects is not without its problems. The most obvious is the reduced experience of students, teachers, and administrators who leave the school during the final 2 years of the project, or who arrive in the school after the project has been running for a year or more; and then there is the normal movement of students from location to location around the country. They may be involved for just 1 year or 2, and then become immersed in another school that may not have a WSP up and running, or may be involved with a quite different project.

Obviously there will be some diminution of the educational benefits of the project for the student who is involved for just a portion of the time, but he or she *will* benefit, and the majority of the students will receive the full benefit. So while it is hard to see how such projects can be managed without these reduced benefits for some students some of the time, the benefits to them and the greater benefits to all the other students is not an adequate reason not to run a WSP. Consider the set of benefits listed earlier, and note that many of them will accrue in significant degree even to those students who experience only a part of a project.

On presenting this proposal to colleagues and school principals, one sometimes receives the counterproposal that these projects should be open-ended. This suggestion has had at least two arguments made on its behalf. First is that no particular terminus be set because the logic of the theme itself and its exploration should set the term for it, not some arbitrary deadline. Some WSPs might begin to wear thin toward the end of the 2nd year, and it would make sense to conclude them at that point, while others might be becoming increasingly rich and exciting toward the end of the 3rd year, and so should be continued for as long as seemed productive. Of course, there is the possibility of some classes or subgroups finding the topic wearing thin, while for others it becomes richer and more exciting. What then? Well, it would be easy to come up with endless possible scenarios at this point, so I will return to this potential problem when discussing the organization of the WSP in Chapter 4.

Second, some suggested that a particular local theme of sufficient richness might be a continuing resource to enhance students' education throughout their careers in the school. So, for example, a school close to a desert area could have as a continuing WSP the study of the flora and fauna of the desert. Whatever else the students in that school might learn of mathematics and history and science, they would, all of them, learn a great deal about the desert. That expertise would become something the school would be known for—building community and invigorating learning—with the added expectation that this large-scale project would enrich and intermingle with the rest of the curriculum.

Well, there is no point being dogmatic about the time to be allotted for the WSP. More reasons will be given later for adhering to the 3-year scale, with the 1-year gap between projects, but there may be peculiar or unexpected conditions that might interfere with the "ideal" 3-year span. And it may indeed be that in some cases successful conclusion of the project might require a further semester or two, or a semester or two less. But there seem to be a number of good reasons to set a term for the WSP, rather than leaving it open-ended.

One of the benefits of the fixed 3-year term is that it gives a "sense of an ending" (Kermode, 1966). Frank Kermode, in his brilliant and insightful short book, shows how meaning is tied in complex ways to our sense of the unit of time we conceive events occurring within—that is, there are no given units in the flow of time, but we create such units to allot meanings to the events that fill them. Our sense of an ending gives us an understanding of the constituents of the whole, and shapes our thinking, feeling, and action about them. The knowledge that the project will end in 3 years may seem like an arbitrary condition, but it is one that will give a sense of possibilities, will help determine the scale and depth of our explorations, will shape what may be realistically expected to be achieved as the product of the work, and will guide how time and energies should be allotted. The ending will also be influenced by the common sense of teachers who, after 3 years, know best the needs of the students and can sculpt the most suitable ending for the project.

Another reason for limiting the scale to 3 years is one touched on above: I think there might be the danger of staleness setting in if it is planned to go longer. Also, the problem of students arriving after the project has begun or leaving before it is completed will be compounded. A further danger in leaving the term open-ended, or as a continuous project that becomes a part of the school's identity—as in the example of the flora and fauna of the desert—is that a central purpose of WSPs is to offer a greater variety of learning experiences to students.

A danger of the ongoing project is that it will itself become absorbed into the routines of the school. This could happen, especially for the teachers, who will find themselves hauling out again the fieldtrip notes on the insects' interactions with cactuses. When such things are repeated many times, they lack the spontaneity and freshness that occurs when the teachers are discovering such things along with the students. But, having said all that, I should say again, the 3-year project is not to be taken as a dogmatic insistence, but rather as a term that recommends itself as offering the best balance of educational benefits against administrative and other potential problems.

No doubt the reader will have gathered that WSPs are not being proposed as something to be tried now and then and here and there. This recommended pattern is for a 3-year project, a 1-year gap for celebration of the past project and planning for the next, and then another 3-year project. I am proposing WSPs as permanent features of the experience of schooling for students, and as a permanent addition to the curriculum.

Initially, no school is likely to take on WSPs as a new and permanent feature of their program. Perhaps if enough administrators, teachers, students, and parents think a WSP might be worth a try, we may see a pilot project implemented, perhaps planned so that it can conclude after 1 year if it seems not to be delivering what is promised in terms of community building and learning. At some point in the spring of the 1st year a decision might be taken to let it run for a 2nd year, or not. But it is hard to see why some schools would not commit to giving the idea a full trial, and launch into a 3-year WSP. Decisions about whether to follow the pattern recommended—of a gap year and then launching a new project on a different topic—will obviously turn on the general perception of the success of the first attempt.

Obviously no school is going to commit to this permanent revolution without trials and pilot programs and studying how such projects have fared elsewhere and also perhaps for the more conservative, the development of significant support materials for those implementing the projects. But the educational value of WSPs is potentially such that their adoption as an addition to regular schooling is the intended long-term purpose of this proposal.

THE WHOLE SCHOOL PROJECT TOPIC AND ITS PRODUCT

Choosing the topic for the WSP is clearly crucial. The topic will have to have wide buy-in by all the stakeholders. If the choice is some local and dramatic geological feature, then the choice may not present a problem and little dissent. But if the whole world is open for the selection of the topic, as indeed it is, then settling on a suitable one may be a bit of a challenge. Chapter 4 will address this challenge by laying out the criteria that should determine the topic chosen. But even following these criteria, or choosing among those that will emerge as suitable examples, will leave a task that will not always be easy to manage.

The topic will have to have richness and diversity and yet a clearly delineated border. It should also yield during its exploration and discovery uses for the full range of curricular skills students are to learn during these years. It must involve opportunities for mathematics to be used in learning something important about it—precise measurements, careful counting and estimating quantities, assessing volume and quantifying diversity, and so on. Scientific methods should allow us to discover important facts about it—quantities of water absorbed by flora, consumed by fauna, and escaped as run-off, seasonal effects that can be detected and measured, experiments that can be devised to show insect or animal or plant behaviors in different conditions and locations, and so on. Historical dimensions should expose deeper meaning—the effects of earliest habitation that can still be detected, how human purposes have shaped the flora and fauna, influences of pollution that are evident and of what kind from what activities, and so on. And there should be opportunities for students to use artistic techniques and skills both to represent what they have learned and also to learn through, as they investigate some features of the topic aesthetically.

This aesthetic component, though mentioned last here, should not be considered least important. Deliberate thought needs to be given to evoking students' sense of wonder and awe at central features of the topic. If we fail to engage students' sense of wonder with the project, then its educational value is going to be marginal. A large-scale enterprise is not worth launching into if it is to be seen as just a varied form of learning utilitarian knowledge and skills. It has to capture the emotions, imagination, sense of wonder, and sense of awe—or we are missing the educational point of WSPs. The claim that WSPs can "invigorate learning" is not meant as simply a method of teaching something more efficiently, in the sense of some simple-minded notion of quantified chunks of knowledge memorized for specific quantities of time; the invigoration comes from evoking levels of meaning and understanding that routine teaching rarely reaches, and that ride on engaging students' imaginations in the topic (Egan, Judson, & Cant, 2013).

The topics chosen will always need to be explored from many disciplinary perspectives, but also an important feature of WSPs is that they will be seen in an interdisciplinary way. The product is not to be conceived as an accumulation of a set of more or less discrete disciplinary contributions. Rather, we need to make clear that although each discipline has something to add and expose about the topic, the topic is also a whole. While science, math, and history may provide different perspectives on the flora and fauna of the desert, the reality is not divided. Our ways of seeing are to be distinguished from what is seen, as far as we can manage this. I will discuss the topics and their selection in more detail in Chapter 4, but I do want to indicate here that one important purpose of the WSP is to involve all areas of the curriculum in the project, and also emphasize that this does not exclude the crucial importance of engaging students' imaginations and sense of wonder with the topic.

Another important feature of planning each WSP is specification of the main product of the work. From the beginning it must be clear that the students will not simply be learning about—to use our recurring example—the flora and fauna of the desert, but that all they learn will find a place in some final product and presentational form. The final product will need to be chosen carefully, because it will shape many of the activities involved in the project. If, for example, the product is to be a comprehensive set of webpages, some of the students' work will be different than if the product is imagined as a book or a mural or a performance.

The product is, of course, a product of the educational experiences of the students and teachers, but it should also be conceived as having a further educational value to those who will view it, read it, or watch it. That is, the public at large, politicians, or other groups will also benefit educationally from the finished product, and this dimension should be kept in mind during the planning phase. Some thought about what format might best serve this further educational purpose is appropriate at the beginning.

Again, there's no point in being too dogmatic about any of these suggestions for how WSPs might best be planned and organized. Some flexibility and contingencies need to be a part of any project, and of these large-scale projects perhaps more than most. If, for example, the plan is to produce a three-dimensional mural and some discovery made in the process of the work can be dramatically shown via a video taken at the time, then some accommodation of such serendipitous but significant discoveries will sensibly be made. (Perhaps in that case it isn't difficult to imagine a segment of the mural cleared for one or more looping video displays, along with changing slide shows, etc.) In fact, we expect that most projects will lead to a multimedia product. But, even so, the variety of forms multi-media products can take needs to be considered carefully at the beginning, so that a relatively clear expectation of the finished form can give direction and guidance to the activities planned by particular classes during the project. Each class activity through the 3 years needs to have a clear sense of how their immediate work is contributing to the accumulating whole.

INITIATING WHOLE SCHOOL PROJECTS: AT WHAT GRADES?

Previously I suggested that a K–12 school could adopt a WSP, and all students at every grade could take part. I even suggested that a separate elementary school might share a topic with a nearby middle school and/ or a high school, and they could work together for the 3 years. This might seem fanciful to some, and, indeed, the prodigies of organization and management that would be required in some places might be beyond school personnel. I want to mention this possibility so that it is not simply dismissed, but might be considered if circumstances conspire to help make it possible. It would be a pity to lose the educational values of multiage levels working together if WSPs are implemented.

But, for the most part and very likely for the first instances, WSPs will be implemented in individual schools, and will consequently have different characters and topics determined by the grade level of the students. So, we will likely see elementary schools with their own WSP, and separate middle schools with theirs. A number of educators who have discussed this proposal claim that it will be rare for high schools to implement a WSP. It's not the lack of educational value, but rather that the pressures of exams and an increasingly less flexible curriculum in the higher grades simply doesn't allow the curricular space to accommodate such a long-term project that will not feed directly into increasingly urgent vocational or academic needs. But it may well be worth high school administrators' pondering whether a WSP might not enable them to meet some of their urgent objectives as well or better than their current organization. Note that the first example in the following chapter is of a high school's implementation of a WSP.

Depending on the grade-level range that will be involved in the WSP, many of the variables mentioned here and below will have to be adjusted—not greatly, but obviously some accommodation will be needed, from the choice of topic to the resulting product. Even if the WSP does involve a whole K–12 school, or a cooperating set of schools, the skills of the students at different ages need to be borne prominently in mind in both planning and process. For that reason, Chapter 7 is dedicated to exploring learning principles and engaging imaginations in WSPs. The learning principles change depending on the age of the students, as do the principles that can guide how we engage their imaginations at different ages.

Helmuth von Moltke famously noted, "No battle plan ever survives contact with the enemy." Not wanting to consider school personnel in any sense the enemy (!), the same might be said about any educational theory or innovative project. While WSPs are new, they are not without the smaller-scale precedents evident in the kind of projects I mentioned earlier. Even so, questions about whether they will work better for separate primary, middle, and high schools or for more diverse age groups working together from different local schools—or even, given developments in communications technology, different schools in different locations or even countries—or about what local conditions may favor them or hinder them, and so on, will have to wait on experience. My goal here is simply to lay out the principles that seem likeliest to produce the greatest educational value.

WHOLE SCHOOL PROJECT PLANNING

All educational activities require careful planning, but a complex 3-year-long whole school project will require its own distinctive form of planning. Chapter 6 will be devoted to examining the process of planning a WSP in some detail, but I will describe here some features of what administrators and teachers will be taking on.

No WSP is going to happen without a few people in the school being convinced of the educational value of such projects and who are themselves committed to making the project work in their own institution. These are the initiators. The first step is a commitment to setting up a WSP, shared by possibly a small number of teachers and administrators, which leads to informal discussion, and that can include many others in the school. The next step will require that a more formal committee be organized, willing to spend time exploring the possibility of introducing a WSP to the school. Their work will involve assessing the resources needed for the project to be accepted and put into action, and will involve deciding on a timeline of steps, which will be described in more detail later. They will also need to explore possible topics, maybe short-listing two or three. Somewhere in this preliminary process presentations will need to be made to the rest of the school community—teachers, administrators, students, parents, and any affected members of the community—both to describe what will be involved and to solicit their views and advice about the process.

If this is the first WSP being broached, then this step may be made early in the fall of the year prior to the planned beginning in September of the following year. Let us assume that general agreement is reached to give it a try. No doubt, assurances will need to be given to skeptics that the project can be stopped early if it proves unable to deliver on the educational promises made on its behalf.

A somewhat larger committee will now need to be formed for the remainder of the year prior to the beginning of the WSP. This committee will need prominent representation of the school administration, a financial official of the school, two or three teachers and students, and possibly representatives from parents and the wider community. The committee will be involved with the occasionally intricate tasks of ensuring that every student and teacher be able to explore some aspect of the project and interact with others, such that they all learn the fruits of one another's work. This is the phase of planning that I will describe in Chapter 6.

CHAPTER 3

What Whole School Projects Look Like: Three Examples

The Qingdao garden comes along.

Instead of exploring in detail how WSPs can be organized and implemented, I will first provide some examples of what such projects look like in action in different schools. And to do this in a way that will exhibit the greatest authenticity, I have asked the people who have been involved in organizing and implementing them to describe what they did and what resulted. I will look in varying degrees of detail at three current projects, giving most space and detail to one in Oregon. The first is from a school in China, then one in Canada, concluding with the detailed examination of the planning and implementation of the WSP in the Corbett School in Oregon.

In this last example, the principal will set the context, describing the school and its setting, and how the project got under way, followed by accounts from three teachers about how they did their own preparation and made it all happen. The reader should be alerted to the fact that the teachers who made this project work became so interested in the topic that they put more planning and preparing than would normally be necessary. It is possible to put a WSP into operation with a lot less work, but this kind of enthusiasm does seem to be a WSP contagion!

This book lays out in some detail an ideal for a WSP, but the reader may notice, in some of the examples that follow, how local contingencies or practical constraints lead to some deviations from the ideal. Clearly these examples give evidence of the educational value of the program, and small differences from the book's orthodoxy may always be inevitable.

QINGDAO SECONDARY SCHOOL

As the name suggests, this school is in Qingdao, China. The school offers a dual Chinese-Canadian high school program. Like all such offshore schools, Computerised Quantity Surveying Services (CQSS) offers a dual program, and CQSS students are considered members of both the Canadian program and the host school. The host school serves a much larger student population, around 3,000 students in grades 8–12, with around 200 teachers. In the morning and early afternoon students attend British Columbia, Canada, curriculum classes. The courses are taught in English by British Columbia (BC) certified teachers. In the late afternoon and evening, Chinese courses are offered. These follow the local Shandong Province curriculum and are taught in Mandarin. The programs are certified by both the BC Ministry of Education and the Shandong Bureau of Education, and are intended for Chinese students planning to enter Canadian universities. CQSS serves a relatively small school community of some 130 students in grades 10–12. The staff includes eight BC certified teachers, as well as a BC certified vice principal and principal. The school is located on the south campus of Qingdao No. 9 Secondary School, a key public high school in the city of Qingdao. The city, which boasts a population of around 7 million, is noted for its temperate climate, clean air, and fresh seafood. Qingdao is generally acknowledged as one of the most "livable" cities in China.

The account that follows is written by the principal, Yvan Zebroff. After consulting with students and teachers, Yvan chose as the topic "Garden plants of Qingdao" for reasons that will become clear in his description of the planning process. One reason is connected to the school's location in a highly urbanized environment, which has benefitted and suffered from rapid development in recent decades. Yvan also teaches in the school, so he is qualified to describe ways in which the WSP can be incorporated into regular teaching that satisfies the school curriculum requirements and external curriculum standards. Although the WSP is only completing its 2nd year as of this writing, it helps give a useful image of a project in action. Yvan describes the WSP as follows.

The Topic

Before the winter break, I met with colleagues to discuss the idea of implementing a WSP (based on the description on the webpage: www.ierg.net/wsp). The reception to the idea was positive. Teachers could see potential benefits for the school, particularly in terms of exposing students to activities and interests otherwise inaccessible to them. As expected, teachers of academic subjects expressed a bit of apprehension about fitting a WSP into the curriculum (i.e., given the perceived need to complete textbooks, unit exams, and prepare for provincial exams, etc.). But all agreed to incorporate a WSP into their courses when possible and applicable.

During our meeting, we brainstormed potential areas of study and narrowed these down to three topics, but we failed to reach a consensus during the meeting. I volunteered to take some time over the winter holidays to select a topic (one that addresses the needs presented in the meeting, and meets the criteria set out on the WSP website).

I opted for a natural world topic, as the natural world is most glaringly absent from much of the curriculum, and from students' experience in general. Knowledge of flora, when presented in the science curriculum, is distant and abstract. Plants are missing in a physical sense as well (one would be hard-pressed to find more than a handful on the school campus). Even the plants students consume at lunch are usually altered beyond recognition. In short, I hoped such a natural world topic might help create a relationship that is currently lacking.

Some of the teachers had suggested making the school garden the topic for our WSP, and this would indeed make a fine product, but I thought it lacked the complexity necessary for a WSP topic. On the other hand, exploring all the flora of Qingdao, as some other teachers suggested, would probably be too vast an undertaking. As an alternative and a compromise, I settled on "Garden plants of Qingdao." I felt this topic could capture the narrative of human–plant interaction over time. Importantly, the focus would be on the plants (and their stories) rather than the economic benefit they offer (though this too would surely be explored). It seemed also of particular educational importance in an area that has seen significant devastation of local plant life in the drive for economic development.

The topic is sufficiently complex. Indeed, it is complex enough to be broken down into various subtopics: medicinal herbs, spices, flowers, ground crops, and so on. Also, many school subject areas could be used in exploring these topics: for example, math, biology, botany, history, anthropology, literature, fine arts, and so on. Undoubtedly, many of our prescribed learning outcomes could be addressed.

The Product

This WSP was designed to have two final products. In 3 years' time, the school will develop a school garden that includes a variety of indigenous and domesticated plants, including flowers, medicinal herbs, spices, ground crops, and vines. In addition, we will publish a book documenting the experience and demonstrating the various understandings gained about these plants. All participants (students and teachers) will receive the book following the final presentation to community leaders and parents. I hope that both the garden and book will have a lasting value for our school community.

Of course, various other (subject-specific) products will be created over the 3-year period. In producing the website and the book, students will utilize and develop a range of conceptual skills including, not least, an ecological awareness, drawing on the ideas, techniques, and support materials available on the related website (www.ierg.net/iee).

1st Year

Newsletters and webpages have been used to document the project's progress. By the end of the 2nd year, we should have in place a complete website dedicated to the project. In addition to these Internet tools, students will prepare year-end presentations about the project.

As an example of incorporating the WSP into various subjects in the school, I am teaching a "Planning 10" course this year. Through the Planning curriculum, students learn about vocational focus areas. By grade 12, they are to select one of these and create a graduation transitions portfolio. In short, students decide what they would like to study after graduation and begin preparing for this. In practice, the curriculum does not evoke a great deal of enthusiasm (on the part of students or teachers). I sense the WSP as an opportunity to "invigorate learning" in this course.

I will offer students an opportunity to use a variety of focus areas (e.g., art and design, media, humanities, technology, science and applied science, health, foods, recreation) in exploring the WSP topic. Individual work produced for the WSP can be added to students' graduation transitions portfolios. By grade 11, students will need to choose one focus area to develop in greater detail. For example a student might develop general skills of art and design through his or her work on the WSP. By grade 12, students should develop expertise within their focus areas. Hence, the artist might work specifically with watercolors (e.g., painting various medicinal herbs). Importantly, as students gain expertise, they will share their understandings with others. Such interaction will occur within and across grade levels (e.g., the media group might run a workshop on creating a short film about the domestication of rice; science students might give a lesson on utilizing the scientific method to assess various weeding methods, and so forth).

So the "Garden plants of Qingdao" Whole School Project is up and running. It took a bit of arm-twisting but we (a few student representatives and I) finally convinced the local school board to do a bit of excavating. The garden area we had selected happened to contain some rather sizeable boulders, as well as various construction materials buried under the surface. However, all of this was eventually removed and suitable soil brought in.

The first day of planting was the tough part. The rest has been good fun. The kids and I have begun researching and planting and sowing in earnest. Trees and grass came first. Now we have started with some of the flowers and herbs. We will begin planting some of the vegetables later this week. (Qingdao is remarkably cool this spring, so everything is a bit late.) Grapes will come last. Students have taken on various roles (managers, artists, reporters, scientists, writers) and each is busy on particular projects that will later be used for the website. Many of these projects focus on particular cognitive tools (author's note: See Chapter 7).

2nd Year

The school is growing and so is the garden. In this, the school's 2nd year, the garden project was divided in two: Some students focused on planting and maintaining potted plants, while the others focused on planting and maintaining garden plots. Both sets of students connected their work in the garden to one of five career focus areas: (1) Humanities, (2) Art and Design, (3) Science, (4) Media and Technology, and (5) Business Administration. These focus areas connect with a number of school curricula. In working on the WSP, students are also able to add individual work produced in the WSP to their graduation transitions portfolios.

In my class, students were introduced to and were given the opportunity to select a particular career focus area. The class decided to focus on planting medicinal flowers and herbs in pots. Research projects were conducted on the herbs and their uses. Seeds were selected and sowed indoors in early spring. In summer, the potted plants were taken outside and placed on the south-facing wall adjacent to the garden plots. Groups of student volunteers alternated in watering and weeding the plants. Individual students also worked on their particular focus area in Planning 10. The work produced will be added to graduation transitions portfolios and will be showcased on the school WSP website.

Other students are continuing to work on their individual focus areas. The work is becoming more specialized. In addition to individualized work, the art and design group developed a garden mural as part of their Art Foundations 11 curriculum. The media and technology group has begun work on the school website, and has begun compiling necessary material to this end. Science students and teachers have taken on a number of projects, including the development of a system for creating compost for the garden from cafeteria waste. Students also researched and selected a natural fertilizer to help enrich the soil. After first considering kelp, they opted for fermented rapeseed husks, a fertilizer that is readily available and widely used by local gardeners. Both projects will be included on the website. The business group has considered ways of improving the garden. Most notably the group has successfully campaigned for the addition of a wall to protect the garden from a nearby refuse area.

Additional developments: Green thumbs are contagious. An unexpected benefit of this WSP has been the extent to which it has engendered greater connections with the large Chinese host school that houses our program. Teachers and students of the host school regularly come to work on the garden project. Host school administrators, teachers, and support staff regularly give valuable advice and support to the project. This year, such interest has led the host school to develop its own cafeteria garden on the campus grounds. The cafeteria garden now produces seasonal, organically grown produce for the school's lunch program.

It may be of interest to indicate how the WSP is integrated into other subjects in the curriculum. Figure 3.1 presents a sample. (Photographs of the development of the garden are available at www.ierg.net/wsp/case-studies/canada-qingdao-secondary-school/.)

Figure 3.1. Sample Schedule

ESL 10 (Jigsaw assignment)	SCIENCE 10 (Ecology Unit project)	PLANNING 10 (Occupations Unit)	ART 11 (Mural design)	GRADUATION TRANSITIONS
In groups, each student selects a different garden plant to research. The information gained is used to compose the plant's "autobiography." Autobiographies are presented in one of several possible formats: for example, as a "prezi," film, graphic story, oral interview, or narrative poem.	"Symbiotic Relationships in the Garden." As part of their unit on ecology, students create a poster on one of the symbiotic relationships in the garden.	Students select one of five career focus areas (1.) Humanities, (2.) Art and Design, (3.) Science, (4.) Media and Technology; and, (5.) Business Administration. Focus area groups consider work done in the garden, work that still needs to be done, as well as new ideas for improvement. Work is divided and roles are selected. Students develop individualized plans of action, as well as a rubric for assessing their performance.	Students are introduced to mural painting. Groups begin sketching ideas for mural design.	Grade 11: Student volunteers join the Planning 10 class and assist grade 10 students in the focus areas. Grade 12: Students continue working on WSP presentations. These will be given to the school community at the end of the school year.

WESTWOOD ELEMENTARY SCHOOL

Westwood School is in Coquitlam, BC, Canada. The total number of students is approximately 210. There are nine enrolling teachers plus at least another 10 teaching staff in a variety of positions, from ESL, librarian, resource room, counselor, and so on. In addition, there are four support staff, and the principal, who spends a portion of his time teaching. The school is generally regarded as "needy" within a low-socioeconomic pocket in Port Coquitlam. Westwood is one of 45 elementary schools in Coquitlam, the third largest school district in BC, Canada.

Taken from the school's APL (Action Plan for Learning):

"Westwood Elementary School is a very diverse student community with an enrollment of approximately 210 students. Enrollment numbers fluctuate throughout the year, as a certain segment of the parent community is somewhat transient. Students come to Westwood from a variety of single-family homes, townhomes, and social-housing, as well as several community daycare/preschools. Our school qualifies for Community Link funding from the district. These funds are used to support our vulnerable students."

This account is contributed by Jonathan Sclater, the teacher who was instrumental in promoting the project and helping to get it going, and by Pamela Hagen, who had been involved from the beginning with Jonathan and took over the project when he moved to another school. They both worked with a number of colleagues. Jonathan's blog from early in the project begins:

At Westwood we started our 3-year WSP called "Respecting Our River, Embracing Our Space," which is about the Coquitlam River that runs nearby our school. Students will be engaged in spending time at the river location itself, and learning about various aspects of our local ecosystem, such as native plant and animal species. We also have a number of school grounds and building improvement plans related to this. Students have had input in designing a new entrance to the school as a river walkway, and we are looking into a variety of grounds improvements. (We already celebrated a tree-planting at the front of the school in late September.) We also have a number of plans for the interior space of our school. For example, we are gathering the students together to name the various wings of our school as tributaries of the river and to discuss what other features of the river can inspire artwork, murals, collaborative work, and so on.

What is really interesting is how having a project like "The River" has got everyone so excited. My hope in suggesting this was that we would involve community members in the planning of this project. We already have a local artist who wants to lend her expertise and is joining us in our next planning session. I guess I can't call it *the* project—I definitely know it's not *my* project—I think the best term reflects the fact that it has become *our* project; it will belong to the students and their families, the teachers, and the community. I am beginning to realize that when you have a good idea and everyone is working together on it, good things will happen. It is amazing to me how a network happens when you get to see it from the roots. People just really want to be a part of something where their voices can be heard and share their idea toward a common goal.

A main reason that I am continuing to think and plan around a central idea is that I am beginning to see this approach as an important part of the forming of our school identity and culture. The students start to care about their project, and they start to form an attachment to the space we occupy together, and more important, they start to relate more to one another.

According to the WSP philosophy, WSPs deliberately celebrate diversity among students, and recognize the value of many kinds of contribution by seeing how each can bring to a common project abilities and skills that no student would have been able to bring alone. "The River" is not intended to be a limited study with facts to be memorized and then quickly forgotten. Instead, "The River" will be a springboard to much larger possibilities. The intent of a WSP is to focus on the topic for 3 years. This will allow for the development of understanding that cannot be achieved in only 1 year. The river is not dry and dead, but vibrant and alive (well, okay, it is a nonliving, renewable resource, but you get the idea). There will be some obvious connections to parts of the curriculum (habitats, animals, water, resources, an so on). And there are ways to help generate the "flow" of ideas beyond our local community. What are rivers like in other places? What is there to learn about the oldest and longest rivers, like the Nile? The Ganges, for example, can hold a very spiritual and cultural importance to many families. What do communities do that lack necessities such as clean running water? There are innumerable local and global possibilities for making this a meaningful topic to study, because it will lead to something greater than any individual effort, and it will move us beyond the walls of our own school to reach out to the community. There can be many cultural and personal connections that students will be able to bring in and learn about.

Here are some basics we considered when planning:

1. Orient yourself toward the topic/project: What do we know and not know about it? Who can help?
2. Manage the information in a way that makes sense for you and your group. You can't tackle it all at once.
3. Consider the community of learners around you: How can we reach out beyond our walls? Constant reflection about why you are doing this is critical to the project's success.

So why would anyone want to take on this added work? Yes, it will stretch us out of our comfort zones, but isn't that what we always want for our students—that they are willing to take some risks and try something new? How better to teach such things than by exemplifying them? We do this because we know that is where the most learning can happen. I am excited and a little nervous about this adventure with my colleagues, but I know it will be much greater than anything I have ever accomplished in my teaching on my own!

Pamela Hagen writes:

During the 2nd year of the 3-year plan, a grant application to the BC-based group Art Start was successful to provide funds to enable us to go to work on some of the environment transforming ideas we had. We arranged meetings with a local community-based artist who would work with the staff and students to help with the changes to the school, to enable us to bring to visual life a sense of bringing the river into the school. This included making the entrance to the school more inviting and welcoming by having students' river-themed designs incorporated into painting the entrance walkway.

The values underpinning the WSP at Westwood Elementary are continuing to be reinforced through "River Cards" being awarded to students who exemplify the values of Respect, Imagination, Valiant Effort, Empathy, and Responsibility—hence, RIVER. Students whose River Cards are drawn from those awarded each week, have their names and achievements announced on the school public address system at the end of each week, thereby reinforcing the values and theme of "The River" project.

Student-designed signs have been mounted in the various wings of the school with the names of each of the three wings: Salmon Creek, Stoney Creek, and Cherry Blossom Creek. These names were chosen by students to reflect the location of the school with regard to the river itself. Various specific rooms in each wing have been given specific names—for example, the Computer Room has been renamed "Electric Current."

The organizing committee was re-formed to include staff members new to the school at the start of the 2nd year. What continues to be important for the staff is that through the WSP cohesion and camaraderie among staff members and between staff and students transcends routines of planning and organization.

The new committee and solicitation of further ideas and directions for the WSP has brought the school community more tightly together, and has laid a foundation for expansion during the 2nd year to further involve parents and the wider school community. At the same time, however, staff members are free to individually pursue aspects of particular interest under the auspices of the project. For example, the raising of chum salmon from eggs in a special tank set up in a common area of the school is being led by one staff member. This exciting display allows the students' multifaceted appreciation and connection among formal school subjects, environmental considerations, and their community, including local First Nations groups.

As the project continues to move ahead, initial ideas from year 1 are being revisited, fine-tuned, and carried out where possible in year 2, thus providing an ongoing framework that allows contributions from new staff members and students while maintaining the integrity, core values, and beliefs underpinning the project. There is ample opportunity for the voices of all parties, especially the students, to be heard and acted upon; it becomes *our* school, not just school!

One of the things that strongly impresses me about this experience is the sense of togetherness around the school that transcends the systematic and small political problems that seem to overwhelm us at times. Somehow the WSP seems separate from all of that "stuff."

How Does the WSP Fit into the Regular Block Schedule of the School?

The problem with answering this question is the complex relationship between the WSP and the regular timetable. The WSP is an overarching "framework" or context within which the curriculum functions. Therefore, even though one might wish to create a timetable/ block schedule about WSP, it may not be possible. Also, one term or semester is not necessarily the same as the next because there are different curricula subjects and responsibilities that need to be fulfilled. For example, during the 1st year of the WSP, in language arts when teaching about the writing of different forms of poetry, students were asked to focus some of their writing on the theme of "The River," with different forms of poetry about river topics. Art was brought in with the decoration and design of the poetry booklet cover. In addition, during that term a large part of the science curriculum was related to "The River," such as the development of the ability to do multifaceted science observations, including use of the senses of smell (the rotting flesh of dying/spawning salmon), hearing (the changing sounds as we came closer to the river and then at the river with birds coming to feast on the dying salmon, plus the sounds of rain and the water), and sight (visual changes in the greenery around the river in the fall). We also introduced some mathematics by checking the temperature of the water and using statistics to make general counts of the number of salmon appearing in the river over a period of time. Often connection between a curriculum topic and the WSP was more casual or fortuitous—an individual teacher would see an easy way to connect with the WSP and benefitted from the greater enthusiasm of the students extending their knowledge of the river and finding the curriculum topic more meaningful.

Who Were the Main Organizers of the WSP in the School?

In preparing the WSP prior to year 1 and in year 2, WSP activities were coordinated by Jonathan Sclater, assisted by Pamela Hagen and Chealsy Fraser. Partway through year 2, after the departure of Jonathan Sclater (to another school), Pamela Hagen took over coordination of WSP; Chealsy Fraser also left shortly after the start of year 2 (maternity leave). At the start of year 2, two new staff members volunteered to come on to the WSP committee: Kerri Johnston, who has an environmental education background, and Cristina Lupien, who has extensive experience in horticulture.

Pamela Hagen coordinates and brings various elements of the project together. Both Kerri Johnston and Cristina Lupien meet and discuss the project on a regular basis with Pamela, and help present the committee's suggestions to staff at regular staff meetings and solicit the staff's further suggestions about how they can incorporate their curriculum requirements into the WSP. Drawing from their own backgrounds and experience, Kerri and Cristina are fine-tuning the plans as we approach each phase of the project. With the overall structure/framework of the plan agreed upon, there is still enough fluidity to use whatever talents and interests committee members bring to the "table," and also to draw on the talents of other staff members.

I will conclude with a set of slides (Figure 3.1) Jonathan prepared for a conference presentation about WSPs. They sum up the ideas and activities very well. (Photographs of the development of the river project are available at http://www.ierg.net/wsp/case-studies/westwood/.)

Figure 3.1. River Whole School Project Slides

The River is about ~

- Building community and moving beyond the classroom walls . . .

  Building relationships and developing a deeper understanding of something doesn't always need to involve an actual school building.

- Gaining respect, awareness, and understanding for our world and how we interact with it.

Origins of Our River WSProject

There were many ideas that "floated" around about the product we will create with the students:

- a mural in the front foyer area showing the river and the plants & animals that are part of the ecosystem,

- painting the ceiling tiles one after the other down each wing of the school so it looked like a river flowing overhead,

- outside we can create nature spaces like rolling grass hills with paths of stones for kids to play on that bring the elements of the river to us.

Year One:
School Building Improvements

- Front entrance river painted on walkway (from street to main doors). Work with students to develop designs for the front walkway/entrance area.

- Painted river theme continued on walls down each wing leading to classrooms. Artwork of animals, plants, and rocks on walls. Each wing to be named as a tributary of the river.

- Bring the salmon tank into the school so we can raise the salmon eggs and then release the fry into the River.

- Participate in the World Walk to Water Day in 2013. Students can walk to the River, collect some water, and bring it back to water the plants at Westwood.

Year Two:
School Grounds Improvements

- Landscape improvements to kindergarten area in front, front hedge by entrance, back grass area—rolling hills.

- Continue school building improvements by adding student artwork of river animals to roof peaks.

- Outdoor seating area improvements with a mosaic tile project covering outdoor tables with student designs of flowers, plants, fish . . .

Year Three:
Community Connections

- Taking care of the river through walks and clean-ups. Inquire with the City of Poco about planting flowers along the river paths.

- Fundraising and awareness for local charities such as homeless shelters, SHARE, as a connection to community members who are less fortunate and live along the river boundaries.

- Include grade 8 helpers from Maple Creek to run a "Nature Club" at lunch time and help to maintain our nature spaces.

- Involving our Aboriginal Education support workers in art projects and learning about the River and the animals from Aboriginal Elders.

Reasons for Our WSP

Let us not lose sight of the fact that ... *the product is only the visible outward expression of the process* that we are going to undertake with our students at Westwood.

What is really exciting is to see all of us (teachers) getting excited about something together and the "flow" of ideas when working together. This WSP will allow us to make many connections and there is the potential to create many "bridges" over our River.

CORBETT CHARTER SCHOOL

Corbett Charter School is a K–12 school near Portland, Oregon, with approximately 400 students. Despite being a community school that draws students from a wide variety of socioeconomic backgrounds, it is known for some astonishing academic achievements. Over half of all enrolled students in each grade typically pass an Advanced Placement exam. This is over 11 times the rate at which graduating seniors statewide achieve the same result. Corbett Charter High School was ranked number three among public high schools in the nation by the *Washington Post* in 2011, number two in 2012, number four in 2013, and number three in 2014. The reason? Unparalleled opportunity for rigorous, college-preparatory coursework.

Corbett School is close to the Columbia River Gorge, and so the school chose the gorge as its WSP topic. This description is introduced by the school principal, Bob Dunton, and described in more detail by three of the teachers who were engaged in making the WSP happen—Sheri Dunton, Lindy Sims, and Alyssa Reed-Stuewe. Here is Bob's introduction:

To walk through the doors of Corbett Elementary School is to enter a conspicuously dedicated space. A single, broad corridor stretches the length of the 400-student building, and the mural on its walls represents, to scale, the Columbia River Gorge from The Dalles to Troutdale.

The professionally painted landscape is punctuated with student-made plaques representing flora, wildlife, and human activities along the river. Hand-painted salmon, some realistic, some fantastic, are suspended from the ceiling.

The "Columbia River Gorge Initiative" began as an attempt to invigorate an elementary program that was searching for an identity. The elementary school was, by all standard measures, effective but not remarkable. All standard measures, as it turns out, make it very difficult for one elementary program to distinguish itself from hundreds of others.

But even though the elementary program rightly saw itself as the bedrock for the successful achievements of students in the upper grades, there was no recognition beyond the recurring thanks and support of the district. And beyond the question of recognition, there was a nagging sense that the elementary school lacked an organizing principle. It lacked a focus for the talents of its staff and students. It lacked fire—we wanted to "invigorate learning and build community" in the school.

So the "Columbia River Gorge Initiative" was born out of two motives, one immediate and one longer-term. The immediate question was how to put Corbett Grade School on the map and gain it the respect (and support) that it deserved? The second, larger question was how could we better prepare students for the challenges of Corbett middle and high schools, which were very demanding programs?

Its perch on the rim of the Columbia River Gorge affords Corbett unique access to a region that is rightly considered a national scenic treasure. The origins of the Gorge in geological cataclysms spanning thousands of years; the primacy of the Columbia River Basin in the cultural, economic, and physical geography of the region; and the sheer spectacle of the local landscape made the Gorge worthy of years of intense interdisciplinary study, and promised lessons that would readily transfer to future studies.

Following the pattern for WSPs, the teachers determined that the Columbia River Gorge curriculum would be delivered in a 3-year cycle: The history of the Gorge, the plants and animals of the Gorge, and the geology of the Gorge. The 3-year cycle would allow each student to encounter each area of the curriculum twice: once while studying using the learning tools described in Chapter 6 for the first years, and then a second time using the next set of learning tools.

The remarkable story of the Gorge's formation, well told, is a drama immediately worthy of the attention of young learners. Telling any story well requires an intimate understanding of its constituent events;

sustaining that story across months and years requires substantial learning. What began as a planning meeting to discuss how we might present the formation of the Gorge became a program for introducing students to the formation of our solar system to include the formation, composition, structure, and dynamics of our rocky planet Earth!

Oregon is a geological marvel, consisting largely of scrapings from the subducted floor of the Pacific Plate, augmented by consecutive lava flows, punctuated with volcanic eruptions, and sculpted by mammoth Ice Age floods.

The Columbia River Gorge breaches the Northern Cascade Mountain Range, creating the only viable transportation route from western Oregon to the central and eastern regions of the state. A drive through the gorge is a remarkable experience in diversity. Distinct climatic zones, wildlife, and flora slip by at a remarkable rate. A drive along the Columbia reveals a historic dam, navigational locks, fish ladders, and fixed stations from which Native American people still exercise their traditional rights to harvest salmon. The Columbia, which within the Gorge constitutes the boundary between Oregon and Washington states, crosses county lines and city limits, and is under the jurisdiction of the Columbia Gorge Commission, a federally authorized agency with representation from both Oregon and Washington.

It is important to note that Corbett Charter School is an Imaginative Education program (cf. www.ierg.net). This orientation profoundly impacts our approach to the study of the Columbia River Gorge. Although the Gorge is literally right outside their windows, Corbett teachers approach it as an exotic marvel and come at it by way of the nebular event that gave birth to our solar system. This is decidedly not an "expanding concentric circle" approach to the curriculum! Proximity doesn't have to mean commonplace or taken-for-granted.

Proximity is, however, cost-effective. Our students have benefited from any number of day trips into the Gorge, where they have sat in longhouses, paddled canoes, traversed Bonneville Dam, toured the fish hatchery, hiked to waterfalls, and inventoried indigenous plants.

What follows are accounts from three teachers, with input from several others, of the implementation of our Whole School Project. The variations in their accounts, in terms of style, approach, and activities, reflect a decentralized process in which teachers had substantial latitude and responsibility for the development of the project. The other caution that should perhaps be inserted for the reader who may be considering implementing a WSP is that they should not be too daunted by the amount of energetic work these teachers put into preparing the project. Two points might be made: First, these are undoubtedly a group of unusually dedicated and talented teachers, willing to spend significant time above and beyond what would be considered normal; and, second, once the commitment to a WSP topic is made, it does provide a stimulus to invigorating learning and building community among teachers as well as students, so some extra commitment from what is routine in schools might reasonably be expected once a WSP is under way.

WHOLE SCHOOL PROJECT PLANNING SUMMARY FOR
PRIMARY GRADES: THE SOLAR SYSTEM AND GEOLOGY

by Sheri Dunton

Corbett Charter School primary classrooms engaged in a broad study of the solar system, the geologic history of the Earth, and the geology of Oregon during the 1st year of the WSP. This curriculum was developed by Corbett Charter School primary teachers as a part of an ongoing Whole School Project in a 3-year curriculum rotation. The project is focused on developing student expertise regarding the Columbia River Gorge. For the primary grades, instruction is planned and implemented according to the first set of learning tools (described in Chapter 6), elaborated further on the Imaginative Education Research Group website (www. ierg.net). No prepared curriculum or kits were used. All curriculum was prepared and designed as part of the ongoing WSP. The general planning strategy for this 1st year's curriculum involved all the K–3 teachers in as much of the planning process as possible in order to reflect the best ideas and to build the emotional engagement of the teachers themselves with all parts of the plan.

The elementary staff of Corbett Charter School met in the spring of the year prior to beginning the project in order to review a 3-year science and social studies curriculum rotation. The goal of this meeting was to review the rotation in light of the Columbia River Gorge WSP project with an opportunity to make changes and to develop an initial framework for the next school year's curriculum. The teams came out of the planning day with a commitment to a broad curriculum rotation plan, direction for summer research plans, and an initial supplies and materials list.

The K–3 primary staff chose a curriculum plan that began with a study of the solar system followed by an overview of the geologic history of the Earth and of Oregon, as a foundation for learning the geology of the Columbia River Gorge. We would take a "Google Earth" approach, zooming in through space and time, introducing concepts that form the foundations of geology.

Because none of the primary teachers had more than the most basic recollection of geology and the geologic history of the Gorge, we began building our content knowledge by reviewing literature and sharing books for a course of summer reading. We took fieldtrips, using books on Northwest geology or online resources as guides. We also began to think more specifically about framing units on the solar system to begin the school year. Teachers exchanged emails sharing references and we met on several occasions for 2- to 3-hour planning sessions over coffee to share information and ideas for shaping the content to draw on the first set of learning tools.

We continued reading and note-taking to further develop content knowledge, writing poetry and stories for classroom use, researching photographs and video clips online, and locating songs and poems to support the content. All the materials were found or developed by the primary teachers. I should add that we did find this joint exploration and preparation energizing for ourselves, and we also felt some excitement that we were preparing something from which the students were going to get a great deal of knowledge and pleasure.

Corbett Charter School teachers developed an ongoing relationship with the naturalist serving Oxbow Regional Park over the year. He agreed to work with us to develop a custom fieldtrip that specifically complemented our geology curriculum. In order to plan a custom fieldtrip, teachers spent 4 hours one Friday visiting the park. We toured the park to view and discuss geology exposures, curriculum, and activities with two naturalists.

Since fieldwork forms the backbone of geologic study, many geology articles and publications are organized to discuss geologic exposures along a fieldtrip route. Local geology fieldtrips were detailed in articles and papers published online. We prepared a document including photographs of interesting geologic exposures with commentary to share with teachers and parents. We also developed materials for classroom use to complement the fieldtrip.

Teachers within this small primary planning group have worked together throughout the year. The focus on the Gorge and our pulling materials, ideas, and lessons together as a group provided a new and rich dimension to our activities as teachers. The students were not the only ones to enjoy and benefit from the WSP!

THE GEOLOGY OF THE COLUMBIA RIVER GORGE

by Lindy Sims

Planning, researching, and teaching our "Living and Nonliving Resources of the Columbia River Gorge" unit took just over a year. The unit is part of a 3-year rotation of curriculum and was developed using the middle years learning tools (described in Chapter 6).

Our team of five teachers, representing both Corbett Charter School and Corbett Grade School, sat down in April and had our first planning meeting. This meeting took about 2 hours. We had decided to study our Gorge's geologic history for the first part of the year. The main two questions driving our discussion were: "What is heroic about doing geology?" and "Where is the story?" The ideas of mystery and detective work were suggested by the ways that geologists take clues from the land and uncover the past. Much like a detective, a geologist must be curious, resourceful, and determined. Like all scientists, a geologist must believe in herself or himself in order to present new ideas to a conventional-minded community.

Between April and August, our team went back and forth between research and planning. We divided up the work in libraries, at bookstores, and online, taking pages of notes and reading anything and everything we could get our hands on. That summer, our team read books such as *The Magnificent Gateway* by John Eliot Allen, *Cataclysms on the Columbia* by John Eliot Allen and Marjorie Burns, *On the Trail of the Ice Age Floods* by Bruce Bjornstad, and others. We read about Alfred Wegener and plate tectonics, and J. Harlen Bretz and the Missoula Floods. Through our research emerged the stories of Wegener and Bretz: adventurer detectives who were curious, resourceful, and determined. Our own growing excitement about the topic made us increasingly confident, as we located heroic characters and great stories, that the students would also become emotionally and imaginatively engaged in the WSP.

We also looked for local experts and organizations. We needed help from people who could point us toward unique geologic sites and local evidence of the Missoula Floods. We intended to pay to join the Geological Society of the Oregon Country, and go on its fieldtrip that focused on local evidence of the Missoula Floods, but the man leading the fieldtrip happened to be the neighbor of a teacher on our team! We got in touch with him, and he graciously offered to take a group of teachers on a fieldtrip. In August, we spent a day exploring the Gorge, with the help of our very knowledgeable guide.

Once the school year began, our team met for at least 1 hour per week, formally and informally in the hallways. These meetings were designed to keep each teacher focused on the larger narrative and framework. We wrote songs, raps, and poems to help students memorize the basics of geology and become geologists themselves. We worked to keep our narrative in mind and to be purposeful about the use of the sets of learning tools. In summary, we were bewitched by what we had learned and, after the planning period, were ready to bewitch our students with the astonishing Columbia River Gorge.

PLANTS AND ANIMALS OF THE GORGE

by Alyssa Reed-Stuewe

Nestled atop the extremely windy, Douglas fir–lined Corbett Hill on the Oregon side of the Columbia River Gorge, Corbett School and Corbett Charter School have access to miles of riparian zone, dripping temperate

rain forest, stunning creeks and waterfalls, and, of course, the mighty Columbia River. In this section, I will describe how we studied the plants
and animals of the Columbia River Gorge.

Our team met for about an hour on a planning day the week before school began. My partners had already brainstormed a long list of
potential plant and animal topics and had begun fitting them into a cal-
endar. In an effort to dive more deeply into a few subjects, rather than
surveying a great number, we ended up slimming down a bulleted list
to plants and animals related to the layers of the forest: salmon, insects,
amphibians, mammals, birds of prey, trees, shrubs, ground cover, fungi,
and edible and medicinal plants. We also began to discuss how these
diverse topics are connected by food webs, nutrient cycles, and cycles of
decomposition, conflagration, and renewal.

The most important piece of our initial conversation was determining a starting point. I want the curriculum I create to respond to my
students' needs and interests, as well as to the unique and unpredictable
classroom culture, and, of course, I also want to create new interests for
my students. Beginning with something engaging is very important. A
father of one of our students was connected with an outdoor school and
had access to a salmon-raising program. This opportunity to provide a
living, breathing visualization of a totem Gorge animal was too good
to pass up. We would begin with the heroic story of the salmon, as we
raised real salmon in our own classrooms, watching them hatch and develop into fry.

We split up our classes into three teams so that each kindergarten–
2nd-grade child could have an older buddy in 3rd–5th grade. We took
these buddy teams and divided them equally into three teacher-led
grade villages. We planned to swap so that our students could interact
and learn together in these village groups a few times a week, or as our
curriculum dictated.

This particular age range of 5- to 12-year-olds, meant that we would
need to draw on both the first and the second learning toolkits (mentioned in Chapter 6). The first toolkit includes use of binary oppositions,
songs, storytelling, games, engaging images, and metaphor. The second
toolkit makes use of a newly developing literate eye, heroes in narrative,
and graphic organizers to arrange their thoughts. Designing a unit based
on mystery also engages young romantics on a quest, where they are
empowered to solve a problem.

At the end of our initial meeting, we chose our roles in planning
initial celebrations to get our students excited to work together within

the content. Each of us spent time over the next few weeks gathering materials, designing instruction, and coordinating spaces for our kick-off event——a salmon celebration. At this event, students made salmon-themed bookmarks and nametags, buddies gave one another gifts and ate snacks. We worked with amazing parent volunteers to get us fish tanks with thermometers and 250 orange salmon eggs, which soon had little eyes and began hatching into alevin.

A small amount of my time, perhaps 2 hours broken into chunks, was spent writing a brief narrative entitled "Sammy the Salmon," in which the heroic salmon faces the many dangers of swimming upstream (such as black bears, eagles, fishermen, and waterfalls), so he can return to the place of his birth, fight with other salmon, spawn, and, very heroically, die. This narrative was intended to be simple enough to be told aloud to the children, with the children participating in the telling through movement and dramatic play. The short time I took to put together a very open narrative became hours of strongly engaging curriculum. The children were able to raise questions, gain confidence with the details of a salmon's migration, and experience this part of the salmon's life cycle in terms of a binary opposition: survival or destruction.

We spent a few hours collecting and organizing written materials to teach about the life cycle of the salmon. The elder buddies would be responsible for reading materials and collecting notes and information to teach the younger buddies. The younger buddies would be responsible for artwork and some note-taking. Our villages worked together a few times a week, playing games, doing research, and making banners representing each stage of the life cycle.

Through semiregular weekly lunch or after-school meetings, usually lasting 1 to 2 hours, we shared our contributions to the curriculum, reflected on their efficacy, and determined our next direction. We selected plants as our next topic. We focused on the forest layers: canopy, understory or shrub layer, and forest floor. Each member of the team took a layer and endeavored to prepare four to six lessons' worth of activities for the villages, drawing on the sets of learning tools. The public library and the Internet were important sources for front-loading, research materials, lesson plan ideas, and graphic organizers.

I enjoyed my time as a researcher, because I followed my curiosity. I became fascinated by moss, denizen of the forest floor, as well as the decomposers that inhabit it. I learned about the charming tardigrade, or waterbear, a tiny relative of the terrific velvet worm. Waterbears are fascinatingly diverse microorganisms. They come in many shapes and sizes, with different numbers of legs and antennae. They eat the moss they live in or other microscopic organisms. I also became fascinated by the variety of local fungi and their anatomy, as well as by the curious habits and life cycle of slime mold. I made a comic book of the life cycle of the fearsome, alien-like slime mold, which the children illustrated and captioned. I integrated into the waterbear imagery extreme facts and an activity where they could imagine themselves to be waterbears, designing their own antennae, number of legs, and personalized prey. We all had a lot of fun.

We decided to choose a few species of animals to focus on for the spring, and also to invite a student teacher and some charter school colleagues to join our think-tank. We chose birds of prey and designed a unit on predator and prey relationships between mammals. I worked on the concept of metamorphosis to draw parallels between six species of butterflies and six amphibians. These last few units were intended to be a few weeks, rather than days, long. They are where our imaginative work really began to flow into engaging, content-rich lessons that led our students to experience, question, and think critically about the content. Over a few weeks of discussing and exploring pictorial, film, and written materials, buddies created raptor trading cards and participated in a *Guinness Book of World Records*–style raptor award ceremony.

We also prepared a spectacular mammals unit on the idea of tracking wild animals. The unit began with a visit by a professional tracker and a look at the learning tools, including observation skills, which a tracker brings from his world to the world of the wild. They created rotating predator-prey kits for each participating classroom, using video clips, informational books, tracking guides, and poems and stories about the mammals involved.

Our metamorphosis unit drew from the emotional engagement that a metamorphosis is a nearly miraculous event, and we used the binary opposites of freedom versus constraint and stability versus change. A voracious caterpillar eats and grows monstrously, then freezes into a seemingly still pupa, within which his entire body is breaking down and reforming into a new creature. Finally, a delicate winged butterfly emerges, dries his wings, and flies away to begin the cycle anew. Tadpoles are aquatic, gilled creatures, much like fish in that they must live underwater. Growing legs and lungs, they are able to escape the constraint of their nursery ponds and freely hunt insects on land! I distributed mealworms and appropriate habitats to participating teachers, so children could handle, predict, and observe them as they pupated and hatched into darkling beetles. We collected images and made fact sheets for the 12 species of insects and amphibian we would study. We put together a journal for organizing information on the life cycles of these animals, and collected related fairytales and video clips of metamorphosing insects and amphibians.

The WSP, at least the way we did it, was extremely engaging for the teachers and resulted in enthusiastic participation by the learners.

CHAPTER 4

Choosing Topics and Criteria for Whole School Projects

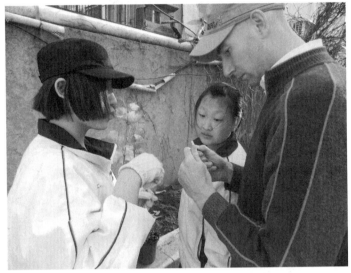

Principal consults with students about planting.

I begin this chapter by saying two seemingly contradictory things: Choosing the topic well is crucial to the success of the WSP, and it doesn't really matter what the topic is in order to attain the educational benefits a WSP can deliver. The seeming contradiction can be resolved by recognizing that while the *particular* topic is not important, the *kind* of topic chosen is crucial; if we get the kind of topic right, then a large range of particular topics can do the job for us. So let's begin by getting clear on what kind of topic we need for a successful WSP.

CRITERIA FOR CHOOSING WSP TOPICS

The goal of the first part of this chapter is to articulate a set of criteria that will provide guidance in choosing particular topics for particular places at particular times. These criteria will need to be made explicit and clear to the whole community involved in the planning, and they should help make this crucial step as easy and uncontentious as possible. The second part of the chapter will be given over to discussing particular suitable topics.

Stakeholder Agreement

The first criterion for choosing a topic will be fairly straightforward. Whichever topic is chosen *must attract the agreement of all the stakeholders*. In most cases, such as our examples in the previous chapter, this isn't likely to be much of a problem. As long as everyone involved can see genuine educational value in the topic, and it satisfies the other criteria below, most reasonable people will be ready to give it a go. However, I can imagine situations where competing groups get behind pet topics, and rhetorically pitched battles make contentious what ought to be a pleasant negotiation. Although such problems will likely occur rarely, planning groups are advised to be prepared for possible contentiousness, and be careful to select a topic that will not be likely to encourage it.

Complexity

A second obvious criterion is that the topic *must be sufficiently complex that it can sustain 3 years of study and exploration by possibly hundreds of people*. One of the aims of the WSP is to help everyone involved see that many people working together can achieve a large-scale product, so the chosen topic has to be amenable to a variety of broad and also intensely particular inquiries. In general, this seems to incline toward natural world topics; or, if a school wants to explore a human-made topic, it must have rich dimensions—historical, cultural, aesthetic, strategic, and so forth, to explore. (One of the examples discussed later imagines a school near Ludlow Castle in England first choosing the castle for its topic. Though there might be enough richness and diversity in that single castle to satisfy their needs, depending in some degree on their chosen product, I nevertheless anticipate that castles more widely interpreted might constitute a better topic, even though the local one could be the focus of special study and exploration. In that case, there are around Ludlow many castles within easy fieldtrip distance, so perhaps the set of local castles might be the finally chosen topic.) In general, the criterion of adequate complexity needs to be met whether the topic is natural world, human-made, or some mix.

Even topics that are the subject of hundreds or even thousands of books—for instance, ants or elephants—may not be sufficiently diverse to sustain a 3-year WSP. How would many different classes do different work that would add significantly to the whole, and what would be a large-scale final product for such a study? Yes, it is possible to imagine how someone might ingeniously manage it, but the WSP is difficult enough to organize without adding to them from the beginning.

A rider to this criterion: The topic must also be sufficiently varied in ways that are generally accessible to all students. What I have in mind is the problem created by topics that might be diverse but are so in ways that require a lot of technical knowledge to grasp much of that diversity. So "subatomic particles" or "the rings of Saturn" or "ancient pottery" or similar topics that require a lot of technical knowledge to really get in the game might prudently be avoided.

Three-Year Completion

Another obvious criterion is that the product decided on for the topic *can be completed in 3 years*. That is, selection of the topic can't be separated from the decision about the product aimed at. There's no point selecting a topic that might be rich and diverse if no one can imagine what kind of product might be constructed and if it cannot be completed in the 3-year period. This shouldn't be seen as too constricting a criterion, however. No matter how intensively a school works at studying, exploring, and experimenting with the flora and fauna of the desert, they will never be able to learn everything. *The trick is to imagine from the beginning a good way to display the product of one's work at the end.*

This doesn't mean that one has to plan it in great detail, but simply that one can imagine a way of representing all the parts of what is to be studied. In significant degree, details of that final product will be shaped and determined while one is working through the project. If it is a mural, then the scale, shape, constituents, and so on will be determined significantly by the explorations and the smaller-scale products that groups of students come up with. What they need to know from the beginning, though, is that the available space for the mural is sufficient to display what the whole school is going to learn and be able to express.

The chosen product, then, should not deform or restrict the work going into learning about the project. Too small a space for the mural would quickly become a problem, and a multimedia product with inadequate provision made for the technical skills necessary to incorporate much of the experimental and exploratory work is also going to be inadequate. Some flexibility will always be required, but from the beginning it needs to be obvious that the topic and its product both define what will adequately occupy the whole school for 3 years.

Defined Unit

Drawing on Frank Kermode's (1966) "sense of an ending" earlier, I suggested that specifying a unit of some kind is crucial to determining meaning. Therefore, a further criterion is that the topic chosen specifies something that *is clearly comprehensible as a defined unit*. This criterion might call into question one of the examples casually used earlier—the flora and fauna of the desert. What desert? There are many kinds of desert in the world, and the flora and fauna of some are quite unlike those of others. Even if all deserts suffer a water deficit, the effects of this single condition in the Gobi Desert are quite different from those in the Sonoran Desert of Arizona, which are different again from those in the Atacama Desert. So we need to be more specific, and perhaps indicate a specific desert area for a WSP.

This criterion directs us to look for a topic that is not so vague that the whole it represents cannot be easily comprehended. It would be difficult to imagine, for example, how one could take on a topic like "landscapes," or "animals," or "space," or "buildings," or "art." These are all too complex and cannot be easily comprehended as a whole. Their diversity is so great that one could only aim for a superficial account, and the form of representing it in a final product lacks any obvious guiding definition.

Suitable topics must be dividable into coherent and integrated components that can be worked on independently by different classes, age groups, intelligence levels, and so on. There must be significant parts of the topic that all groups of children can work on. One of the planning tasks of any WSP will be for the committee to provide a breakdown of the topic into parts that can be adopted by groups in the school. This basic organizing act is common to all large-scale projects, from building a bridge, launching a rocket into space, rehearsing an orchestra, to those apparently authentic scenes we see on TV shows where the chief detective organizes her or his resources to handle different aspects of the investigation of a crime. In the case of each WSP, the organizer has to make an assessment of the range of skills available for the work and make sure that each student can make a significant contribution to the whole; the workers responsible for the launch pad and the gantry will use skills quite different from those of the physicists and mathematicians plotting the flight path, but all are necessary and required for a successful launch. In the case of a proposed WSP topic, if it cannot be divided into appropriate kinds of diverse segments for study and exploration, then that will disqualify it as suitable.

Final Product

A fifth criterion concerns the image of the final product. It must be clear from the beginning what the terminus of the WSP is going to be, and that some specific and achievable terminus can be described. This doesn't mean that the initial image need shackle the project, as flexibility is going to be important in many aspects of the 3 years of work, including changing images of how it might conclude; but a condition of setting out on the adventure of a WSP is that one can describe with some clarity what the final product is intended to be. So we need a clear image to begin, even if we might change that image as we go forward with the project.

Enduring Public Value

Another criterion is that *the product must be something that has a public value.* The work is not being done only for its own sake—though that educational value is central—but that it must be of some public value as well. The final product should be conceived from the beginning to have a purpose that is certainly public and perhaps also political. Not political in a narrow partisan sense, but political in the sense of presenting to the public options or ideas for what is possible for the community with regard to the topic, if it is locally focused. So, if the topic is a study of flora and fauna around a hilltop school, the final product will likely entail information about threats to both flora and fauna, and these might give useful information about water resources in the area and threats to them from developments that might be changed for the general community benefit. Perhaps the final presentational form of the product will have a more general educational and aesthetic value for the community at large; so specific days may be set aside for community members—parents, politicians, anyone who cares to come—to visit the mural about the Columbia River

Gorge, or see the multimedia show on castles; or representatives of the school might make a presentation to a local council or state senate committee on issues relevant to their topic. Sometimes the political purpose may be simply to show publicly the importance of something that is often not adequately noticed—the value of a castle to the local economy, the economic as well as aesthetic importance of local arts activities, the degree of local commitment to space exploration, the role of birds in plant propagation, and so on.

Longlasting Value

It is not enough, however, that the product should have public value. A further criterion is that it *must have a enduring value for the school community* as well, in addition to the educational work and its individual benefits for those involved in the 3-year process. It must leave a residue that enriches the school. So it won't be only the students involved in the WSP who will benefit, but it will have residual educational benefits for all students who follow in the school. The residual benefits will not be as great as those for the students involved in the WSP, of course, but a criterion for the selection of the project should be that it also should have these longer-term benefits.

Often the product may be an attractive and accessible display within the school, such as the mural of the Columbia River Gorge, or a multimedia presentation on castles, or an illustrated map of the flow of water in the locality, or a documentary case study of desert life, or whatever. So the initial planning must also involve some concern for what the residue of the product will be. Over the years, of course, if a school does follow the pattern of a new WSP every 4th year, there will be an accumulation of such products. One doesn't imagine a school becoming cluttered with stuff that only gathers dust, but a small amount of thought can ensure that the enrichment from past projects can persist while not becoming either unnoticed displays or a burden on space.

Something New

A final criterion—added a little hesitantly—is that the topic *should involve the discovery of something new*. I would like to add this to avoid WSPs being seen simply as products of massive encyclopedia and Internet searches, with some fieldtrips that confirm what is already known. Rather, it should be *encyclopedic* in the original sense of the word—an all-round education—which will involve not just discoveries for individual students of what others know, but also some component should involve the discovery of things that no one so far knows. Now, this does not have to be a central component of a WSP—I am not imagining each one making significant contributions to human knowledge. But, when thinking about what would be a suitable topic, there should be some reflection on what might be discovered that is not already known. Sometimes this may not be at all obvious at the beginning. What, for example, will the students learn about castles that isn't already known, or what will they learn about the flora and fauna of the local desert that some expert hasn't already written about at length (and might be persuaded to come in and talk to the students about)? But topics like these at least allow the possibility that something new might be turned up by the explorations of many eager searchers. So, this is not a deal-breaking criterion, such that one has to indicate in planning the likelihood of some new discoveries, but rather a criterion to bear in mind that might help choose one topic over another because the one offers this possibility in a way that the other does not, and something everyone can be alert to as the project goes forward.

We have, then, a set of criteria for the choice of topics. As we explore specific topics in some detail, we might find this set being amended, added to, or reduced. But they give us something to guide our choice of the kinds of topics we might select for a WSP. I will work dialectically, with the criteria helping choose topics and reflection on the topics perhaps refining the criteria further. Here are the eight criteria so far identified:

1. attracts commitment from all stakeholders
2. is sufficiently complex that it can sustain 3 years of study and exploration by hundreds of people
3. can be completed in 3 years
4. is not so complex that the unity of the topic cannot be adequately brought into focus
5. can be divided into coherent components that can be worked on independently, and permits the youngest and oldest and the full diversity of students and teachers to make appropriate contributions that satisfy each group and also add something significant to the product
6. can lead to a specific public product of value that can be presented to public bodies/political powers

7. leads to a satisfying enduring product that will enrich the school
8. involves the discovery of something new

These might seem like a challenging set of criteria, but I think we will find many project topics that will satisfy them.

CHOOSING SUITABLE WSP TOPICS

The task here is to examine potential WSP topics in light of the criteria above, and just tug them to and fro, mentally, to see what will serve as good topics to sustain an adequate project over 3 years. The goal for this activity is to generate a set of topics that educators contemplating a WSP might choose from, and serve as a guide to clarify the kind of topic they might decide on for themselves.

One issue I will discuss briefly concerns the relative attractiveness of local topics over more distant and less obviously "relevant" topics. I have, in the examples so far, clearly favored the local with references to the desert for schools in such regions, sheep-farming for others, major local geographical features, and so on. Obviously, if WSPs are going to become a part of a school's normal curriculum, then one can only take on the main local geographical feature once. On the other hand, it is worth considering that choosing a prominent local feature might make an attractive first topic in order to gain experience organizing a WSP. Also, it should be noted that it might be appealing to a school that had a successful WSP based on a local geographic or cultural feature to want to repeat it in subsequent years. The school would become known for providing that particular valued local knowledge and its expertise, making it an attractive distinguishing feature of the school to the local community and to parents.

A school could cycle through local and distant topics, providing variety in the choice of topics and variety in the forms of investigating them as well. This begins to look like a further criterion, though I think it is rather a matter of what makes best sense for an individual school.

People who favor "Place-based Education" (Judson, 2010) will likely see advantages in mostly focusing on features of the local environment for topics. And certainly any locality will have more than a single feature that could form the subject for a WSP. But I will begin with the topic that is the most detailed example discussed in the previous chapter, and test it against our criteria. I will do this initially in a rather literal way, looking at the topic in light of the eight criteria in turn.

A NATURAL WORLD TOPIC

The choice of the Columbia River Gorge for Corbett School seemed at the time a fairly obvious one, and you have seen the kinds of benefits and challenges that this topic gave to its organizers and students. It seems easily to satisfy the first criterion—no one in the school had any reasons not to take on the topic, and the Gorge was already, through simple experience, familiar to everyone in the school. The geological complexity of the Gorge, its amazing prehistory and history, and its varied flora and fauna ensured that it met the second criterion about being sufficiently complex to sustain 3 years of study and exploration by the hundreds who would be involved in the project. Also, it was possible to organize things so that the project could be completed in 3 years, thus satisfying criterion three. The geographical unity of the Gorge limited the topic in a way that everyone could grasp clearly, and the subject matter could be divided into coherent components that allowed everyone to contribute something significant and feel satisfaction about their contributions to the whole project—there were easy ways in which the math teachers and the art teachers and the social and science teachers could see how parts of their mandated curriculum objectives could be met by tying the learning to the study of the Gorge, thus satisfying criteria four and five. The huge mural combined the artists' background representation with the accumulated students' work, and led to a publicly accessible product that recorded the learning attained during the project, creating a remarkable display for visitors to the school, thus satisfying criterion six. That same display, which is a wonder to visitors, is also a magnificent testament to the work by everyone in the school that enriches the environment for all; it serves as a continuing inspiration, and a continuing educational tool for future generations of students. I am unsure how adequately the project satisfies the last criterion—the ambivalently added criterion that the project should aim to discover something new. Certainly this project exposed a huge amount that is new for all who were involved in it and all who see it, beginning with the formation of the planet to present day details of animal life and human settlements. But I am not so sure that it discovered things that no one knew before.

A CULTURAL TOPIC

Let us take another of the possible topics frequently mentioned above—for a school in or around Ludlow in England that might study the castle. In this case, the study will focus on a cultural artifact rather than a natural feature. It might seem the school could choose to make this project a study of castles in general, though that might run into problems with criteria three and four—it threatens to be too complex, as the variety of castles over time and around the world is huge and hugely varied, and adequately studying such a variety and the conditions in which they were built might run into time and scope problems—though possibly not, as the initial task of dividing the topic would ensure that it could be dealt with in varying degrees of generality. Focusing on Ludlow Castle alone might run into the opposite kind of problem in meeting criterion two—there might not be sufficient complexity to keep everyone exploring for 3 years. Perhaps we might focus on Ludlow Castle but also include the other castles in the region built to keep the unruly Welsh out of England—so we can call our WSP "The Castles of the Welsh Marches," as the borderlands were known. There are around 30 appropriate castles in the area that would enrich this topic, while not becoming too many or too complex for a clear product to be designed for the project. Restricting the WSP to this set of castles would mean that the topic need not get out of hand studying castles from other times and places in the world; and so we can satisfy criteria one, two, three, and four.

Exploring Ludlow and other castles can obviously lead to using measurement skills for mathematics and many forms of calculations—how many stones, their weight, and implications for building even a simple piece of the outside wall of the castle, geography and geology classes can explore the quarries that produced the stones, and fieldtrips might gather information about what distances and what obstacles needed to be overcome in bringing them to the building sites. Similarly, it is easy to imagine appropriate studies in all subject areas, and no doubt the ingenuity of students and teachers would uncover many other ways the project can satisfy mandated curriculum learning objectives. Criterion five—dividing the topic into varied parts so that everyone can contribute something—can be adequately satisfied with the varied set of studies and explorations the Marches castles offer.

It is easy to imagine any number of possible public products that might result from this WSP. Models of a number of the castles in their finished and undamaged forms could be connected with a multimedia presentation that incorporates the knowledge gained about the historical background that created the need for the castles, the form of life within the castles, the kinds of food, entertainments, clothing, children's games, defense technology against attacks and sieges, and so on. This product would be available for presentation to outside groups, perhaps including recommendations for specific kinds of care or development of certain castles, and would also enrich the school, making proud all those who contributed their varied talents to it. So studying Ludlow and the other castles of the Welsh Marches seems to satisfy all the first seven criteria.

Something that might satisfy the eighth criterion—that the project should discover something new—might be managed in a number of ways. For example, after its neglect and decay in the latter part of the 17th and early 18th centuries, many stones from Ludlow castle were used in other regional buildings. In some cases it is easy to see these still incorporated, often as foundations or full walls of more contemporary buildings. Students might search out unrecognized stone from the castle in other buildings around. Mind you, because Ludlow suffered much less destruction than many castles in the area, students might have more success exploring villages outside Ludlow itself for remnants of other Marches castles.

* * *

At this point I would like to pause to examine with the reader how the application of the criteria to these two topics can guide us toward other topics that might easily be included. All very well to have an astonishing geological feature like the Columbia River Gorge on the school's doorstep, but what about the local school in a subdivision in a geologically and geographically undistinguished location? And castles are fascinating constructions rich in history and forms of life within and around them, but not so accessible if one's school is in a suburb of Columbus, Ohio, or Winnipeg, or Sydney, or Manchester. How suitable would such a local environment be for a WSP?

A LOCAL NEIGHBORHOOD TOPIC

Let us assume we are in a typical school in a geographically flat and undistinguished area whose original flora has been almost entirely destroyed in the development of the suburban middle-class neighborhood. If the school committee for the WSP sits down with the intention of planning a study of the local neighborhood, how adequately could the criteria so far identified be satisfied? First the committee will need to identify what area is to be included in the WSP—three blocks each side of the school, or the whole catchment area of the school? What range of features of the neighborhood will be suitable for study—transportation patterns, community activities like arts projects and quilting cooperatives, markets, shops, entertainment facilities, policing, music making, craft activities, underground delivery of water and natural gas, sewers, power lines, public festivals, events, holiday activities, the variety of buildings and their purposes, population, settlement history, wild and domesticated animals, varieties of plants and trees, or all of the above, and more? Let's see how far applying the criteria might help us sort out this pile of possibilities.

The first criterion—getting everyone on board—should be no problem. A study of the local neighborhood is fairly routine in many schools and in many curriculum areas. It is hard to think of any reason why such a topic would not be able to get agreement from the whole school. Similarly, the potential complexity of the topic, given just the subset of items listed with little thought in the previous paragraph, is adequate to satisfy criterion two. The third criterion—about completing the project in 3 years—is slightly more problematic. No doubt it is possible to decide on a final product for the topic, although its diversity suggests that specifying this will likely be a challenge, but perhaps no greater challenge than was the case for the Columbia River Gorge WSP. Both have a great deal of diversity, which could be explored for decades; so the terminal product is not easy to specify in detail from the beginning, and adjustments will need to be made as the project moves into its last year. In principle, however, there seems to be no reason why such a WSP cannot meet criterion three adequately.

Satisfying the fourth criterion presents a related challenge. Simply specifying that the WSP is going to involve a study of the local neighborhood might be sufficient for the first and most general level of agreement, but a lot more needs to be specified to bring the unity of the topic into focus. The Gorge helped this task by its geographical unity, and the Marches Castles around Ludlow helped because there is a limited set, the conceptual unity of which is easily grasped. But the unity and limits of the project on our local neighborhood, especially in a suburban area that melds into others on all sides, is not so easy to grasp conceptually.

There will be local boundaries, and/or a clear catchment area for the school, and simply specifying that the project will be within these might be the next step in bringing the complexity under conceptual control. A related step will need to involve trying to specify, if only provisionally at first, what aspects of the neighborhood will be the subject of the WSP. Perhaps the answer, which will also help the planning process, is to specify a set of items that will constitute the focus of exploration and study. A more thoughtful and organized list than that given above, which included everything from quilting to sewers, might well do for the job. So, while criterion four does present a challenge that will be greater for this topic than for many, it is not a challenge that can't be overcome with a bit of thought and a little ingenuity.

Criterion five is rather easier to satisfy. The list of topics already mentioned above could suffice as a basis for dividing the topic to allow everyone to explore some aspect of it in a satisfactory way. After such a list is more thoughtfully made and organized, it will allow components to be selected by various classes over specified periods of time.

Criteria six and seven concern the nature of the product that will be completed at the conclusion of the WSP. The product needs to be something that performs a public role and also something that enriches the school. How can one represent in some tangible form the diversity of knowledge that will have been amassed over 3 years by all the students and teachers working together? It is easy to imagine various multimedia, digitized forms of representation, but it might also help define the project from the beginning to consider other possible forms. Displays of the underground world of the neighborhood could be made either in the form of models or graphic representations or both, and, for either case, the school might enlist local artists to help the students put such displays together. Different segments of the project could also form the chapters of an illustrated book about the neighborhood and, using the possibilities of ebooks, the illustrations could also include animation and video. So, it is not hard to see that the project can satisfy criteria six and seven.

What can we hope to discover that is new about our neighborhood to satisfy criterion eight? In this case there are quite a few possibilities. Studies of transportation patterns might expose changes not seen from earlier official monitoring, surveys of pet ownership might disclose more exotic pets than anyone imagined or knew about, studies of local gardens might expose some new invasive plant species, interviews might indicate changing patterns of entertainment in the community or intentions to change, surveys might also bring forward new ideas for amenities in parks, and so on.

* * *

It appears that studies of local neighborhoods will likely have no difficulty satisfying all the criteria, even though they may still face organizational challenges. So far, then, it looks as though it will be relatively straightforward to use some spectacular feature of one's locality for a WSP or, lacking such features, more routine environments can yield material for equally rich WSPs.

Spectacular local features can be of many kinds. One might study water in Vancouver, Canada, or in Bergen, Norway, or on Maui, Hawaii, or mining in Falun, Sweden, or Kalgoorlie, Western Australia, or Cumberland, Kentucky, or fish and fishing in Akureyri, Iceland, or Grimsby, England, or New Bedford, Massachusetts, and so on. Less spectacular environments can equally offer adequate topics. In addition to the local neighborhood for the suburban school, alternatives might include, for example, woodland, forest, or farmland flora and fauna in schools near such areas, or urban environments and their patterns of work and habitations, and their human, bird, and insect populations, or persistent features of long-established communities and the impacts on them of modern technologies.

But let us suppose a local WSP does not appeal for one reason or another, or that the main local feature has been the subject of a previous WSP and now the school is planning another and wants this time to choose something more distant from the locality. Can one include such topics as space, or more particularly, Mars, or ants, or elephants, or desertification and attempts to combat it, or species at risk, or other features of the world for which there is no immediately accessible experiential sources of knowledge—except, in that list, for the astonishingly ubiquitous ants?

DISTANT "IRRELEVANT" TOPICS

That scare word *irrelevant* is perhaps a good place to begin. It is still a presupposition for many that whatever we introduce to students must be "relevant" to their experience. This has usually meant that there must be some obvious clear connection between the topic and interests students already have, or between experiences they will have had and the new knowledge that is to be introduced. At one level this makes obvious sense, but the way it has commonly been interpreted in education has meant that "relevance" has become an excuse for not imaginatively engaging students in all kinds of features of the world that would and should create new interests for them—which is, after all, one of the purposes of education. What is the relevance of the person with the longest fingernails to the average student in a suburban middle-class school? And yet nearly all students are fascinated by the mass of "irrelevant" information that fills the *Guinness Book of World Records*, and also many young children become fascinated with dinosaurs, witches, and talking rabbits. I needn't raise unnecessary controversies but it seems useful to begin by suggesting that WSPs that focus on topics such as the solar system or elephants should not be immediately dismissed because they are less obviously relevant than the students' neighborhood. A role of education is to make things relevant that were earlier unknown and unconnected with our everyday experience, and often *we can make them directly relevant by focusing on some emotional connection rather than looking for some content association.*

Above I indicated some random topics that might be candidates for WSPs that are distant from students' everyday world. Let us begin by considering space, or more particularly, Mars, or ants, or elephants, or desertification and attempts to combat it, or species at risk. Maybe we can move from these off-the-top-of-the-head topics in the direction of more suitable ones—if these are found wanting in terms of our criteria.

So what about "Space" as a topic? The issues raised by criteria two, three, and four concern the unity and complexity of the topic. We need to be sure that what we decide on has the right scale and the right degree of generality and particularity for a 3-year project. "Space" seems awfully big, and while Mars is pretty big physically, it may be too small for a WSP, at least in the sense that we need considerable diversity of content. But "The Solar System" seems about the right scale, with sufficient complexity, but also not excessive complexity, and it can also form a conceptually clear unit, even if we discover that what constitutes the solar system has been a matter of some dispute—I'm thinking of all those chunks at the far edges of our system, which increasingly, as we learn more about them, are recognized as part of the mass of material captured and revolving around our sun. A difficulty about the choice between "Space" and "The Solar System" is that maybe either one would be suitable, though we would be dealing with less particularity, para-doxically, dealing with "Space." That is, we know so many more details of our solar system, but what is beyond it is not so easy to divide into many subsets of classification for learning by different classes and ability levels, because nearly all the content requires considerable technical expertise, and the limits of "space" still tax the minds of the greatest experts.

How would the solar system fare against our eight criteria? Well, it's certainly the kind of topic that is generally engaging and of sufficient importance that the whole community can sign on to. All students spend some time studying the topic as it is, so its general educational value is beyond dispute. It captures the prosaic interest in knowing where we are in the universe, and something about what those flickering lights in the night sky are that have fascinated humans from the beginning, and it also captures the romantic delight at the discoveries made during the past few centuries and in very recent times that are bringing into our view the astonishing wonders of our local neighborhood in space.

The fact that the solar system is a part of the curriculum already is no reason to resist including such a topic as a WSP. On the one hand, almost every topic anyone could suggest will be touched on in some degree in the regular curriculum, and on the other hand the inclusion of a WSP can remove the need for the usual curriculum focus, and those classes that in the past were dedicated to introducing the solar system can be incorporated into the much more comprehensive exploration during the WSP. So the first criterion—getting everyone on board—is easily met with this topic.

The second criterion—that the topic is sufficiently complex to sustain 3 years of study by a whole school—also seems easily met. The amount of knowledge generated in recent years is enormous, and a lot of it comes with dramatic pictures and heroic ingenuity in exploring objects in the sky that were little more than blobs of light, or not even visible or known, just a few generations ago. I recall, when I was a boy being fascinated with the idea that people might be able to travel into space, that my grandfather was helpless with laughter when I tried to discuss it; the very idea just seemed to him utterly ludicrous, and flying to the moon was as absurd as changing suddenly into a tiger—a comparison he used, after his many years in India.

The third criterion is, for this topic no less than most others, an organizational matter. The trick here is always to be both imaginative and realistic, and flexible, in planning a final product. How will all the knowledge gained during the 3 years of exploration, study, artwork, and

so on accumulate into a display or form of presentation in which everyone's contribution can appear and in which everyone can be proud?
Groups in the school will be able to dwell on this issue before and during the project, and local circumstances might dictate some dramatic
form that can't be predicted beforehand. As a default where nothing
more imaginative comes to mind, some dramatic multimedia compila-
tion of everyone's contributions might serve as the concluding product
for this WSP of the solar system.

Criteria four and five also seem easily satisfied. While the limits
of the solar system are matters of dispute—just what is out there and
where can the solar system be said to end?—there is a clear unity to the
topic and no problem with focus. Also, there is a satisfactory range of
coherent components that groups can work on independently, or semi-
independently: the moons of Saturn or Jupiter, Venus, comets, the asteroid belt, the lakes of Titan, the possible sub-ice oceans of Jupiter's
moon Europa, the dynamic sun, Mars—maybe two or three groups can
explore different features of Mars as we accumulate lots of new knowledge about the planet—and so on.

The public use of the accumulated and organized knowledge is another matter that will challenge the ingenuity and practicality of the
organizers and participants in choosing the topic in the first place and
in deciding the best form for the final product. It is hard to predict
what would be the most suitable form, but no doubt some aspects of
the solar system can be given local display, and the general multimedia
display might form a dramatic focus within the school. Some years ago
on a main street near where I live flags representing the planets were
attached to streetlights according to scale. The sun started the set on
a large flag, and then, a few blocks later there was another flag with a
much smaller image of Mercury, then some blocks later, one of Venus,
and so on, through the set of inner planets and the asteroid belt. But one
then had a long journey before Jupiter appeared, and then much further
before Saturn, and so on. It was a very vivid demonstration of just how
much space there was between the tiny bits of rock, ice, metals, and
gases that form the focus of our attention in the solar system.

Criterion seven is also clearly satisfied with the imaginative choices
mentioned above for the display of the product within the school. Some
care and thought will be required to ensure that the final product about
the solar system enriches the school, and provides an educational experience to those who interact with it. The final criterion, about something
new being discovered or displayed, is oddly not as challenging as it may

seem. One must expect this project not simply to be one in which knowledge is gained only from printed sources and the Internet. During the 3 years, students may be expected to visit and spend time looking through big telescopes and also spend some time with smaller telescopes or binoculars, learning their way around the solar system and working out how to locate our local planets against the background of the galaxy. They will learn to take their own photographs of various bodies, and these will form a part of the final display. We will not expect students to find a new planet or asteroid, but frequent searching can bring something new to light. Every week, in the amateur astronomy magazines, there are small and sometimes big discoveries. It is not so uncommon for an amateur looking at Jupiter, for example, to be the first to spot an asteroid headed for its upper cloud system, or even detect the brightening trail of a comet. In a school, where there will be perhaps thousands of hours logged over 3 years of inspection of the night sky through telescopes, it is not absurd to expect something new might be discovered.

Now we do not need to spend as much time considering other topics in order to establish that "irrelevant" topics can serve as WSPs just as adequately as local topics. In addition to the solar system, previously I mentioned ants or elephants or desertification. Ants might just suffice to meet all the criteria, as there is such a variety of ants all over the world; they have been studied extensively for a long time, and so there is a mass of knowledge about them. Students will be able to study ants themselves in various local environments, so experiential engagement with the topic is possible; different groups could study different kinds of ants and focus on their constructions, their social structures, their transportation of food, and so on. I am a little wary of this topic only because "Ants" is so very particular a study. Would there really be enough variety for the whole school to study this topic for 3 years? I think it is worth considering in the context of that other casual suggestion of elephants. I am less confident that there is enough varied knowledge about elephants, and there are far fewer varieties, and the only local individuals students might meet will be in the artificial and constraining environment of zoos. My suspicion is that "Pachyderms" might make a more adequate topic than "Elephants." Pachyderms include also pigs, rhinoceroses, hippopotami, mammoths, mastodons, wild boars, warthogs, and some other animals. This greater variety might make it easier to meet the criteria. "Ants," I suspect, would work fine as a WSP.

"Desertification," on the face of it, seems able to satisfy all the criteria, despite being for many students in most schools "irrelevant to their everyday experience" in the trivial sense. There are many areas of the world facing desertification, a lot of knowledge about the process, and many suggestions about how to contain and even reverse it in different places. There is a clear focal point to the topic and there is a lot of varied knowledge about it. Also, it has the value of being an important world-scale concern, about which the students may not only gain knowledge but also become involved in by participating in some role that responds to the problem. Some of the same comments might make it easy to jus-tify choosing "Species at Risk" as a suitable topic.

I am wary of suggesting that the more purely "academic" topics, such as "Castles of the Welsh Marches" or "The Solar System," seem to me preferable to topics that can easily lead to social activism, such as "Species at Risk" and "Desertification." I do recognize the energy that can become a part of students' study when they come to recognize the dimension of activism that can result from their work—indeed this is what many teachers see as the important sense of "relevance to their experience." I suppose I am suspicious of premature conviction-forming that can easily occur, for the best of motives. I noted at the beginning the kinds of themes or larger projects that schools sometimes under-take today—ecological sustainability, elimination of drug use, recycling, racial issues, and so forth, and they mostly involve social engagements that contain a more or less explicit ideological element, or lead very easily in the direction of particular ideological commitments. I am not arguing that we should question, for example, ecological sustainability, but rather that such topics can imbue children with a fervor of con-viction that greater knowledge and wider judgment might make more complex and mature and less absolute. On the other hand, maybe this wider understanding is precisely what a WSP can provide. So maybe the solution is not to avoid such topics, but rather for all those involved to be aware of this kind of educational issue and ensure that the greater knowledge students learn does lead to more complex understanding of the many dimensions of the topic. However, having sounded this note of concern, I do recognize that "Desertification" and "Species at Risk" can make entirely suitable WSP topics. Also, of course, taking on a WSP doesn't mean giving up on these socially sensitive initiatives as parts of regular school activities.

This leaves us with a world full of "irrelevant" topics that would seem to easily meet all the criteria sketched so far—and the criteria seem to be holding up quite well as useful guides to what will likely work best as topics for WSPs. "Ocean Life," "Migrating Animals," "Pirates," "Clothing Through History," "Jungles," "Trains and Railroads," and on and on.

WEBSITE SUPPORT

My research group has generated development of a website for WSPs—http://ierg.ca/WSP/—with a section devoted to the criteria developed above and a list of suitable topics in addition to those suggested here. Anyone having a hard time deciding on a suitable topic could go there for further suggestions. We anticipate that the site will be well developed by the time this accumulation of words becomes a book.

CHAPTER 5

Planning and Executing a
Whole School Project

A WSP organizing committee at work.

In organizing a complex WSP one might sensibly look for help from those who are the world's most effective at carrying out varied coordinated tasks to achieve a common purpose—bees and ants. Bees and ants have an overall plan, decentralized control, distributed problem solving, multiple interactions, and they constantly deploy adaptive behavior (Miller, 2010; Seeley, 2010). One area of school activity that has recently experienced significant development is called "distributed leadership" (cf. Hallinger & Heck, 2009), whereby greater efficiency and satisfaction are gained by staff and teachers, and senior administrators do not lose a sense of leadership. Relatedly, "ecological leadership" models draw more from our insect models than have past doctrines of leadership in education (Fullan, 2004). WSPs require significant distribution of leadership roles to make the project effectively enhance each participant's sense of ownership of the project. They also need other features of organization at which ants and bees excel.

Even though the planning process is crucial to the success of a WSP, this chapter will not attempt to describe the process at great length. In part, because the particular topic and circumstances of the school will affect the planning process significantly, and it isn't possible to try to cover all contingencies. Also, I will provide an abbreviated account here because some of the general descriptions of the process have already been covered by the examples in Chapter 3. My goal here is to outline the *principles* of an adequate plan for launching a WSP. One aspect of an adequate plan is procedures for assessing and evaluating it, so I will also suggest how one might go about both formative and summative evaluation of the planned WSP.

Like any good story, setting up a WSP involves a beginning, middle, and an end. I will treat our planning accordingly.

BEGINNING THE WSP

First someone has to have an idea. Someone will have to propose to the leaders of the school that it is worthwhile considering a WSP. That person may be one of the school leaders, or it may be a teacher who has heard of such an initiative elsewhere, or it could be a parent or a student. Next some information needs to be made available to those who will be most involved in deciding whether to take the proposal further. This could be a simple article that describes the theory of WSPs and/or describes the effects WSPs have had on a school or schools elsewhere, or it could be this book, or the WSP website. Maybe someone from a school that is involved in such a WSP or which has completed one might be asked to give a presentation about it. Or a member of the WSP team could be invited to make a presentation and discuss details of organizing such a project. Obviously, it is important that the people involved in making the decision whether to begin a project be well informed about its practical implications and potential educational benefits.

Exploration and Consultation

Let us assume that the initial information-sharing has not turned everyone off the idea (!) and, as school leaders mull over the possibilities of a WSP and discuss it with teachers and students informally, there develops sufficient interest to move to the next step: to make a decision in whatever is the appropriate forum in the school—a whole school meeting, a meeting of teachers and administrators, of department heads and administrators, or privately in the principal's office by the senior administrators—to launch an exploration of what resources and time would be needed. Those charged with this task will be expected to report back within a month or so to the community with their recommendation, and perhaps with recommendations for good topics for the WSP. Or, a principal might simply chat with key members of the teaching staff one day and decide to go for it the next day.

The first step can be best handled by a small group, which might include a senior administrator, a department head, a couple of teachers who have expressed special interest in the idea, and a couple of students. This exploratory group will become better informed about WSPs and their educational value, the practical problems, and costs in terms of time and resources for this particular school. Let us assume that after meeting a few times, and considering the likely benefits and problems associated with a set of potential topics, the planning team fulfills its assignment by reporting back to the appropriate body in the school with the recommendation that the WSP should be taken to the next step.

Assuming that after discussion and weighing the pros and cons, there is support for beginning a WSP on a local environment topic, the next step is to present the proposal to the school community at large, including parents and caregivers. The exploratory team is tasked with spreading information and encouragement like the bees and ants that spread news of a potential benefit through the hive or colony.

It is obvious that the choice and presentation of the topic to the stakeholders is fundamental to the success of the SWP. Whether the topic is local or distant, cultural or natural, it must be engaging to stakeholders. A clear description of a final product or outcome should add to the enthusiasm of the community at large.

I am perhaps making heavy weather of this initial process of ensuring that the stakeholders are on board before beginning. I anticipate that, as in the examples in Chapter 3, much of what may seem a lengthy period of exploration and consultation can actually happen quite quickly with general community support.

Defining Tasks

Before work begins with the students, a supervisory group will need to be formed, which may be the exploratory team extending its role, or a new group may be appointed. This supervisory group will have one further important task in preparing the project. The general topic needs to be broken into chunks, which can become the responsibility of units within the school. In most cases the units will be individual classes, in some cases it will be larger groups, such as the math teachers and their classes, or science teachers and theirs, and so on. The school needs an initial plan such that every teacher and every class has a clear notion of what part of the WSP, and what part of the final product, they will be particularly responsible for. Again, in the abstract this can seem quite daunting. But it is important to remember that the initial plan is both negotiable and somewhat provisional. The supervisory team will not be dictating who does what but will be suggesting how the topic might be broken into parts, and then negotiating with teachers, students, and department heads about who does what. Again, this can be made to sound like something requiring Napoleon's skills in deploying large numbers to a common end, but in practice it is a process that tends to work out quite easily. All teachers have skills in taking topics and deciding how to organize them into parts for instructional purposes. They will bring this skill to bear in negotiation with each other and with the supervisory team. Remember our principles derived from the bees and ants: decentralized control, distributed problem solving, multiple interactions, and constantly deployed adaptive behavior. The supervisory team's job is to help that first process of decentralizing control over the topic, ensuring that overlap of contributions occurs only when intended, and cooperation among groups is facilitated.

Once under way, the teachers will have control of their work with regard to the topic, and most of the coordination can be done informally in the corridors, or over a sandwich or coffee during school hours or some other time. For much of the time classes can operate separately, arranging their own fieldtrips, visits by experts, and so on.

Administrative and Financial Support

The school administration will decide what resources will be given to the supervisory committee to enable them to support and facilitate the WSP. There will be a cost in time for members of the committee, but they should also have control of a budget both for incidental costs and also for technical and other help in preparing webpages for participant groups and for enabling stages of preparation of the final product. The WSP can make a significant contribution to building community and invigorating learning, but it is not intended to be a major cost item for a school. It will cost something, however, and schools and their initial planners need to make a realistic assessment of what they can afford.

THE MIDDLE OF THE WSP

If the preparatory work has been done adequately, the running of the project should largely take care of itself. This doesn't mean there won't be problems of coordination and timing and so on, but the decentralized control, allied with multiple interactions among the participants, should ensure that most problems can be worked out fairly easily. This is, after all, what teachers do constantly in their regular work.

Organizing, Coordinating, and Educating

The supervisory committee will need to keep an eye on how the various participant groups are proceeding toward their goals, and how the gradually accumulating contributions toward the final end product are coming along. Some groups may need a little stimulus now and then, and some groups who have proceeded faster than anticipated can help some who have been less successful. This way of putting it may make it seem as though there is a tight timetable for producing the final product, and while there is a need to ensure that contributions toward that product keep building, it is necessary to constantly bear in mind that the most important work of the WSP is concerned with the students' learning. The use of mathematics in the project, science classes that relate to it, geographical knowledge that gives it context and basis, and so on, will primarily be designed to ensure students learn the math, science, and geography. Not all that they will be learning of those subjects during the time of the WSP will be a direct contribution to its final product. The WSP only takes up a relatively small proportion of school time for each student and teacher; it is only one of many things going on in the school and in learning in each curriculum area; and it is only one part of a much larger curriculum with which students and teachers are engaged.

The supervisory committee might use some of its resources to arrange webpages, wiki pages, class blogs, and other Internet tools for coordination of work on the project. It should be easy to create a general introductory page that could list and give access to all the various components of the WSP and provide some easy visual access to the work so far completed, what is planned, and how the final product is keeping to schedule. With such tools everyone can have a sense of where they are, how others' work is proceeding, and how the project as a whole is moving forward. Such a central source of information can also provide a stimulus to making connections with unplanned or unsuspected work being done by others, discoveries of shared interests, new directions for a number of groups opened up by one group's explorations, and other ways in which groups can adapt to previously unknown ideas, knowledge, and possibilities.

Communication and Expansion of Routines

All groups will be encouraged to recognize the value of keeping in touch with students' parents and caregivers throughout the program. Partly this is simple courtesy, but also it is one of the enlivening features of WSPs and a part of how they can contribute to building community, not just in the school but also with many groups that can thereby become more tightly connected with the school and its educational mission. Newsletters about the developing project can be sent to parents and caregivers and other community members who might have an interest. Maybe the school uses a Facebook page, or Twitter, or whatever electronic social media are available and prominently used by students at the time, for keeping the flow of information open and active. Teachers should obviously encourage family members to talk with their children about the topic and to share any relevant expertise. As will be seen in the examples given in Chapter 3, one of the rich sources of expertise the schools were able to draw on became known through such contacts.

Much of the work of running the project will be familiar to teachers. Their other tasks will involve provision of appropriate resources—books, Internet, objects, experts, and so on. They will also be responsible for teaching various skills necessary for carrying out the variety of forms of investigations the WSP will require. Teachers will also take the lead in their classes to keep the students up-to-date on the work being done by all the other groups in the school, though they may choose to appoint one or more students to help with this task.

Whole School Presentations

One other feature of WSPs that differentiates them from everyday schooling is the importance of presentations at the end of each year. The main purpose of these is to make more evident more vividly than the project website could the progress made to date. The yearly presentation should be a major celebration for the whole school, during which each group will be encouraged to make a vivid display for the rest of the school community of what they have achieved. The students can be helped to tell the story of their part of the project to the rest of the school, with individual students focusing on particular highlights, and featuring displays of their new knowledge through art and drama.

While the presentations have a serious purpose with regard to the WSP, they can also license a little silliness—funny songs or verses about the project, or anecdotes about the weirdest experiences the group has had on a fieldtrip or searching for information, or video of hilarious incidents or peculiar objects encountered: a kind of *Guinness Book of World Records* account of the extremes and oddities discovered so far. At the same time, the humor should not be allowed to drown out the learning and knowledge that are the purpose of the presentation. Also, my suggestion of a single presentation time each year might not always work best. Some schools might find slightly more frequent whole school gatherings to be valuable.

Another stream of activity that needs to be planned for is assessment and evaluation of the WSP. Evaluation will have to occur in both small-scale and large-scale ways, and in informal and formal ways. Evaluation data will be drawn on constantly to calibrate the ongoing process, keeping information flowing to all the groups within the school. Rather than discuss appropriate evaluative activities here and again later, I will deal with them together in the next section.

ENDING OF THE WSP

As the project moves toward its conclusion there will likely be powerful feelings within the school. This is a culmination of 3 years of work by a lot of people, and by this time there will be significant commitment by students and teachers to ensuring that the final product in particular is as fine as they can all make it. Pride in the significant accomplishments so far should be increasing, as well as a growing awareness of just how much each student has learned about the topic of the WSP. One culminating activity will be the final year-end presentations.

These presentations, however, will be on a different scale from those that conclude the 1st and 2nd years of the project. This should be a major event for the school, with invitations to parents, caregivers, local and regional school board officials, local and regional politicians, civic officials, students who might have been involved with the beginning year or so of the project but had to move on to other schools, and whoever else is thought an appropriate audience. The goal is to show the final product in a way that each child can be publicly acknowledged as having played a part, even though not everyone can be involved in the presentation itself. If the final product is in a video or multimedia format, or a complex set of linked webpages, it could be shown as the concluding centerpiece of the presentation. If it is an elaborate website, designed from the contributions of everyone who contributed to the project webpages, then a guided tour around it could be the concluding event. Alternatively, if it is some construction, such as a central hallway in the school that displays the knowledge contributed by all the participants in the project, a tour would be an appropriate concluding event.

In addition, a purposeful review and evaluation of the whole project should be organized for all the participants. In significant degree there will have been formative evaluation of the project throughout. The supervisory committee's monitoring of the project going forward will be like a finger on the pulse, detecting where there might be problems and difficulties, and giving remedial suggestions where necessary. But, in addition to this, their work should also be guided by the criteria developed earlier that laid out the educational benefits of taking on a WSP and also those for determining what would be a fruitful topic for the school. The committee should be observing the progress of the WSP with those criteria of success constantly in mind. So, for the final summative evaluation of the program, there should be available a significant amount of data to work with. In addition, however, the final semester of the program and the subsequent semester after its completion can be used for gathering further data.

One important preliminary point needs to be made about evaluating a WSP. Evaluation data constitute attempts to discover whether and to what degree the program meets its objectives. There are no data to determine whether they are good objectives or whether it achieves those objectives better or worse than other comparable programs in the school because there are no comparable programs. The central objectives of WSPs are new; they are mostly concerned with the effects of introducing a large-scale joint project into an institution in which such events and experiences may not have taken place before. And it is not possible to compare components with other programs, because it is the structural unity of the WSP that gives it accumulating educational force over the period of its activity. And if the recommendation that students should experience a number of these projects through the course of their schooling is followed, the educational benefits of the WSP should be compounded. In the next section I'll consider a wide range of features of WSPs data that can be collected.

There are some very clear ways in which, for nearly everyone, a general evaluation will be evident after the program has been running for some time. It should be obvious whether in general the WSP has been a success or failure. Has the WSP fallen apart and elicited little interest? If that's the case, detailed data will not be required, or may be of interest only to pinpoint what went wrong. Or has the school community at large felt enthused and excited about the WSP, and has it indeed, built community and invigorated learning? If that is the case, then the remaining information to be collected in the evaluation will be useful largely for improving and fine-tuning the next iteration of a WSP.

Let us assume that the WSP has generally gone well. We will require a more thorough evaluation of the degree to which it has met its objectives to enable the school to improve on the experience for some future WSP. How well the chosen topic served the purposes of the 3-year program can also be evaluated. Apart from such basic evaluation, engagement in more qualitative approaches will be desired. The school administration might appreciate the kinds of more synoptic view of the project provided by a chosen critical connoisseur (Eisner, 2001), and even of the dimensions of it that can be exposed by "arts based research" (Barone & Eisner, 2011). Such approaches can help the administration explore how well the WSP contributed to the bigger imaginative experience that the project was intended to generate in students and teachers. It would help also to give the community, and others interested in the experience, a sense of what it looked like in practice.

A group within the school could perform the evaluation, possibly a group with overlapping membership with the supervisory team, or it could be contracted out to a local college or university, or even to a company that does such work reliably. Indeed, perhaps a college or university might have been brought in at the beginning of the planning process with the understanding that it would provide the evaluation as part of its participation. This could be a college or university that is interested in placing student teachers in the school or whose faculty are interested in doing research on the WSP innovation.

A number of the criteria for a successful WSP mentioned below may seem hard to evaluate or assess with any clarity or precision. But, as with many of the most important educational achievements, simple measures are never easily attained (Eisner, 2001). My concern in identifying the educational benefits of WSPs was not, after all, determined by what could be evaluated easily, but rather by what was of educational value. This is not to say that we cannot get clear markers of whether the WSP is being successfully implemented or, at its conclusion, has been a success. The forms of evaluation appropriate to the very various claims made on behalf of WSPs means that the following set will be quite diverse. It will be clear that forms of evaluation used in response to one claim would also be appropriate in providing evidence relevant to some others. I won't keep repeating such items, but will leave it to the reader to recognize that some of the more detailed evaluative procedures suggested can be used in responding to more than one claim.

The WSP was designed to provide the following educational benefits:

Students build an emotional and imaginative engagement in learning about the world and develop pride in the growth of the project.

This is one of those general objectives for the WSP that is of great educational importance but also is not easy to measure or assess. The fact that it isn't easy does not mean it is impossible, or that we cannot identify some clear markers to indicate whether our WSP is successful against this criterion. One of the markers will be whether the students spend any more time outside school working on other topics, related or not to the WSP. Teachers can note examples of students' increased knowledge and interest in topics beyond the curriculum, and note also the degree of energy and enthusiasm they express about the knowledge they have gained. Teachers can also note through the course of the project evidence of emotional or imaginative engagement in the topic itself. This is less simple to discover, but we can get some sense of it from the engagement evident during the lessons: Are the students eager to learn more? Do they check other sources? Do they voluntarily bring in information to classes? Are they obviously engaged? Do they show concern about the fate of flora and fauna or other features of their WSP? Students might be invited to express their feelings about some feature of the WSP, and they might be asked to draw and write about what they found most engaging. Such work will give some evidence about the degree of emotional and imaginative engagement in the topic.

There are other things the teacher can observe that may help assess how imaginatively engaged students are in a lesson. Consider the following features of their "body language" and classroom behaviors. (Thanks to Dawn McArthur for these.)

- facial expression (e.g., smiling, laughing, open eyes, direct eye contact)
- leaning forward toward instructor and/or interactions with other students
- looking at instructor rather than gazing into the distance or elsewhere in room
- physical movement: whole body motion/jitters, might indicate excitement; in contrast, localized jitters (knees, feet, hands) might indicate boredom
- verbal expressions of surprise, wonder, and so on
- verbal expressions of personal experiences related to lessons/ stories
- tone of voice, volume of talking
- questions asked: number of questions (more might indicate increased interest); time lag to response to teacher's questions (shorter time might indicate higher degree of engagement); number of students wanting to respond/asking questions
- voluntary participation in activities
- interrupting to tell stories/examples, number of different types of examples
- focus and intensity of working (measure the time students work without interruption on imaginative tasks)

These are fairly gross observable measures, and their interpretation may not always be reliable (e.g., the student who takes a long time to reply to a question might be thinking about it more deeply and with some emotional engagement; also one needs to be sensitive to cultural differences in body language), but they are observable behaviors that can be monitored to help assess whether this criterion of success is supported.

Even simpler observations can give us further clues: Are the students punctual when dealing with WSP material? How does their attendance and absenteeism on those days compare with other non-WSP days? What is the overall noise level in the classroom, and what "quality" is the noise—that is, is it clearly connected with work, or other things not work related? Are WSP assignments completed on time and done better than other work? Is there evidence of greater variety of different creative solutions/stories for WSP work than regular classwork?

The scale of the product of the WSP is designed to give participants a genuine sense of pride in what they have jointly achieved. While it is not easy to measure degrees of pride, it should be possible to identify some markers of participants' pride in the product. Is the product displayed in a way that draws public attention? Do participants in the WSP ensure that their own names and contributions are identified? Do they talk about it with parents and others more or less than about other school activities? Are public officials, parents and caregivers, local media, and other schools invited to see and respond to the product? Do students and teachers keep and display the representation of the product given to each participant (in whatever form that comes—DVD, photographs, book, and so on)? A questionnaire or interview could include a simple question about whether participants are proud of the product, inviting them to expand on any positive response in order to get a reading of the aspects of the product they feel particular pride in. The questionnaire could also elicit whether or to what degree they feel a shared pride in not only their own work but also that of their fellow contributors.

Students understand the gradual growth of something very big from many small contributions—"a stone upon a stone, a word upon a word."

Part of the difficulty in discovering how adequately the WSP has contributed to this educational goal is that, as described in Chapter 1, the benefit is something fairly intangible that affects the individual after leaving school; in that understanding of how large projects have been put together, and in their greater readiness to engage in taking on large projects in cooperation with others. Gaining evidence about this claim seems likely to happen best at the project's conclusion. One might ask simply whether they had imagined in the beginning that they would be able to achieve something on so large a scale, and whether the contributions of each participant would add up to something so much greater than anyone's individual contribution.

This claim, though, has some features that are more like an analytic truth than an empirically testable criterion of success for a WSP. One could indeed ask participants at the end whether they do better understand this important insight about constructing something big from many small contributions, but there is a sense in which simply participating actively in the process will almost of necessity bring such understanding. Of course it is possible that some students and some teachers in some WSPs might simply fail to gain this understanding, but one would have to conclude that they must have allowed themselves to become dissociated from the process early on. If we see such failures among many participants, clearly the WSP has been unsuccessful, and this lack of success will be evident in much grosser ways than in developing this understanding.

Having said this, however, it is also likely that this seemingly obvious principle—big constructs are composed of many smaller constructs—will be understood at various levels of sophistication and profundity by participants in the WSP. A surface-level understanding suggests the principle is a truism, even trite, but grasping how very large-scale products can be constructed by many diverse pieces gradually coming together can be a quite profound insight into humans' ability to build cities and civilizations, and about bees' and ants' ability to construct their complex societies in hives and colonies. Truly understanding the principle in a profound way as distinct from seeing it as a simple truism is probably one of the differences that enables some people to take on major, complex, and long-term projects while others can never see their way to doing such a thing or knowing how to start. So the success we are hoping for with regard to this criterion is that deeper understanding in the students' future will lead to initiative and action on a larger scale than might otherwise have been thought possible. Success in this can only be measured over the long term, and there are no instruments to uncover degrees of profundity in acquiring this understanding. However, our summative evaluation surveys and interviews might include some question(s) to elicit responses suggestive of this having come as an insight to participants (Stuffelbeam, Madaus, & Kelleghan, 2000).

Students are exposed to new interests and to learning activities they might otherwise not experience.

Whether a WSP would be superior in this regard compared to normal schooling can be fairly easily measured. The reason to expect greater success on this criterion for the WSP school is due to the extended and intensive work on diverse features of a specific topic, but this is a straightforward empirical matter that the evaluation team would easily gather appropriate data about, using methodologies derived from a number of the publications referred to in this section.

Students see how different subjects in school overlap and work together when used in a large-scale interdisciplinary project.

Schools try to include interdisciplinary work and teachers frequently indicate ways in which one subject connects with other things they have studied and learned. WSPs do this routinely and profoundly. In the case of the Columbia River Gorge, it is clear that even while students will be learning about the flora of the region in a biology class, they become increasingly aware as the project goes forward how this knowledge is tied in with the geology of the Gorge and its history, and how the measurements they did in their math class are vital for understanding why and how the plants ecosystem in the Gorge is sustainable, and indeed how all the diverse subtopics they study in various disciplines are parts of what is seen increasingly as a single whole. This criterion seems more like something that cannot fail to succeed if the WSP runs even moderately well. The connections among varied forms of knowledge are built into the way WSPs work. But, as with some of the previous criteria, it is possible to frame questions for a questionnaire or interviews with students to elicit how adequately they recognize this. If the study involves "control groups" in regular schools, one can discover whether the expectation that WSP students will appreciate this better than their peers in regular schools in fact occurs.

Teachers collaborate in integrated planning and teaching with colleagues.

This seems not to require much in the way of detailed evaluative procedures. If this is not happening, the WSP will be in serious danger of collapse, and that will be evident from other markers as well as amounts of collaboration. Collaboration and integrated planning and teaching are more like conditions of the WSP being operational than claims that require separate assessment. However, the committee that guides the WSP would be wise to keep alert to the degree these conditions of a successful WSP are constantly being used. One marker of the success of the project might be to see such collaborations increasing as time goes on and spreading into areas of teachers' work outside the WSP.

Teachers experience a distinctive educational project with distinctive educational activities, in a context of mutual support.

This, too, is more like a condition of the WSP working properly. These benefits to teachers could be evidenced from questionnaires given at the conclusion of each year of the project. Information about teachers' sense of such features of the WSP, specifically, their sense of their collaborative work, can be solicited, and may be useful to the guiding committee. If teachers indicate that they have not considered themselves as engaged in a distinctive project and distinctive activities it would be clear evidence that something is amiss.

Teachers build a deeper sense of how distinct disciplinary perspectives can come together in a large-scale interdisciplinary project.

The comments made about the claim that students will develop more interdisciplinary understanding of the topic than they do about most of the rest of the curriculum, seem relevant for the teachers as well. The annual questionnaire requested of teachers, along with a detailed focus-group discussion among a randomly selected group of teachers, could solicit evidence of this. First, what are the teachers' self-reports on this issue? In addition, the guiding committee might look for indicators in the teacher discussions about the topic that suggest clear interdisciplinary understanding.

Gaining reliable information on such a complex issue is, of course, difficult. It could be that the teachers' own reports of their thinking are the best that can be expected.

WSPs contribute powerfully to community building within the school.

The fact that a school takes on a WSP is usually an indication that there is already a healthy sense of community in a school. It is, however, possible that leaders in a school recognize some problems in the school that would be helped by a better sense of community and that a WSP might be just the tool to do the job. At a basic level it should be fairly clear throughout the life of the project whether it is contributing to a richer sense of community. If most participants seem only to be going through the motions, without any clear sense of being members of a team to whose joint purpose they are contributing, then it will be obvious that this purpose has not been met. Case study evaluations provide more systematic data from parents, students, administrators, and teachers (see Stufflebeam, Madaus, & Kelleghan, 2000, for an account of the various evaluation methodologies that can yield these kinds of data).

With the expectation that in most cases the WSP will have run with growing commitment and interest among the participants, it would be helpful to have markers of community building that tie directly to the project. At the simplest level one could survey a randomly selected group of students on their sense of being more involved with the school and their sense of contributing to some joint project. One could, connectedly, ask each of the teachers about their perceptions of their students' sense of community and understanding of a joint purpose. Schools differ, of course, but in any school it should be possible to establish a set of markers that indicate whether a greater sense of community has been achieved during, and by the conclusion of, the WSP. Such markers might include:

- attendance figures for voluntary school activities—sports, drama, hobbies, band and orchestra, and so on;
- reports by students and teachers, from surveys and/or interviews, of increased cases of supporting others' learning, cooperation in activities, and increased incidence of initiatives;
- student reports of teachers encouraging and supporting their individual work;
- reduction in discipline problems;
- increased reports of students feeling comfortable in the school environment;
- increased parental involvement in the school; and
- improvements in system items such as orderliness in the classroom and school environment and respectful attention to the public spaces of the school (Comer & Haynes, 1992; Epstein, 1995; Fitzpatrick, Sanders, & Worthen, 2010; Grant & Ray, 2009; Henderson & Berla, 1994; Sanders & Sullins, 2005).

Other clearer markers of an increased sense of community might be areas on the WSP website in which community members could make contributions. The evaluators can observe whether such contributions increase over the life of the project in number, quality, and commitment. Similarly there may be other project-related publications, such as a newsletter, that will both reflect back to the community the general work being done, but will also solicit contributions and feedback from the whole community. They may note also whether there are similar small-scale publications on some specific part of the WSP, such as animal life in the desert, daily life in the medieval castle, insects in the neighborhood, and so forth, and whether these are read widely and are contributed to by many students and teachers.

WSPs help students, teachers, and administrators discover how individual contributions to a coherent large-scale project can produce enormous results, helping all participants to feel pride for more than just their own individual work.

Evidence for improvement with regard to this claim during the WSP will in part overlap with some of the markers mentioned above. I noted earlier that the development of a sense of community builds trust in and tolerance of the diversity of its members. One marker of increased appreciation for the ability of others will be increased examples of cooperation, especially among students who might not be "natural" partners, but who find themselves brought together by what they might individually contribute to a part of the WSP. This evidence could come from teacher observations and reports, once they are requested to observe for such behavior. Similarly, teachers might look for, and perhaps encourage as a feature of the WSP, increased incidence of joint initiatives by groups of students. Do teachers encourage and observe over the course of the WSP increased incidence of negotiating of tasks between teacher and class and among students? Do they see increased evidence of sharing tasks, especially in ways that allow for different abilities and interests? Do they see increasing cases of compromising in the sharing of work on parts of the project?

Evaluating whether members of the community do or do not feel pride in the project, and particularly pride in the work of others as well as in their own work, is not easy to measure—but the earlier discussion regarding how one might assess students' pride in the project seem also pertinent here.

> **WSPs encourage appreciation for the abilities of others, enabling everyone involved to recognize that all kinds of learning styles, intelligence, and ability level can play an important part in constructing the whole.**

Seeking evidence for better support of different learning styles, kinds of intelligence, and so on is bedeviled by controversies about what they mean. Recently there has been a flurry of research that has led to denying that "learning styles" exist (cf. Pashler, McDaniel, Rohrer, & Bjork, 2009). The reason people have wanted to explore learning styles and kinds of intelligence and ability level is driven by the assumption that the more we know about these, the better we can tailor instruction to be more effective if "meshed" with the learning style or kind of intelligence of the learner. Unfortunately for this seemingly common sense assumption, there have been two problems. One is definitional. It really hasn't been easy to sort out what such terms as *learning style* or *kind of intelligence* actually mean, nor is it clear what underlying psychological reality they are supposed to refer to. In addition, the belief that using supposed knowledge about students' styles of learning can lead to better instruction has been undermined by a lot of recent research. The Association for Psychological Science commissioned a review of the topic whose results flatly contradicted the popular belief that we can "mesh" such styles or intelligences to instructional methods (Pashler et al., 2009), and studies that look at attempts to match instructional methods to children's learning styles have apparently had no beneficial effect on their learning (Stahl, 2002).

But what is meant in this criterion for successful WSPs is more simple than the heavyweight theoretical and empirical battles being fought about whether claims that learning styles or kinds of intelligence as essential psychological insights can aid education. Rather, our concern here is more about recognizing diversity among students and teachers, and acknowledging that this diversity is something valuable for us to draw on rather than to suppress, and in particular it is something to encourage and support in building an educational product like the conclusion of a WSP. It might be useful to change the wording of the claim to reflect this, but I have decided to keep it because it is currently the common language of educational discourse about evident differences among students. I simply want to acknowledge those differences and suggest that WSPs should lead to greater sensitivity to them as the project goes forward, and acknowledge that those differences are a source of strength in any large-scale joint project. We do tend to give undue weight to a single area of difference among students in education, and label it with the unclear term *intelligence*. Other differences seem less relevant to everyday classroom activities or as irritants to which we have accommodated.

It is hard to measure precisely this suggested change in recognition and appreciation of differences, but the evaluation team should be alert to looking for evidence that teachers and students show appreciation of various diverse contributions, even from those often considered academically the least able students. Explicit questions in surveys can provide information about any increased recognition and valuing of diverse contributions to the project, and the concluding questionnaires and interviews can similarly deliver some evidence.

* * *

The other area of the WSP that we might want to assess is the success or lack of success of the topic chosen. The discussion about suitable topics ended with a set of criteria listed below, which can serve as the basis for evaluation of this aspect of the WSP:

1. attracts commitment from all stakeholders
2. is sufficiently complex that it can sustain 3 years of study and exploration by hundreds of people
3. can be completed in 3 years
4. is not so complex that the unity of the topic cannot be adequately brought into focus
5. can be divided into coherent components that can be worked on independently, and permits the youngest and oldest and the full diversity of students and teachers to make appropriate contributions that satisfy each group and also add something significant to the product
6. can lead to a specific public product of value that can be presented to public bodies/political powers
7. leads to a satisfying product that will enrich the school
8. involves the discovery of something new

These criteria seem easier to gain adequate information about than some of the items in the previous list that indicated objectives for WSPs in general. Many of the evaluation tools mentioned there can be brought to bear on these too, though, in most cases, fairly simple measures will be available. It would be useful to have such results published in some form for people exploring whether to implement a WSP, and we will keep a place on the WSP website for information about how particular topics have performed in practice. It should add to a rapidly growing WSP "best practices" inventory of ideas.

CHAPTER 6

Learning Principles and Engaging Imaginations in Whole School Projects

Engaged in the created garden.

There are two initial challenges to launching a WSP. First, how to engage the various school stakeholders with the idea so that they will commit to it, and, second, how to engage the 5-year-old, the 7-year-old, or the 15-year-old to sustain a commitment to 3 years of study of the Columbia River Gorge or Marches Castles or flora and fauna of the desert or the solar system. The WSP has to appeal to the usual variety of students one finds in a typical school, where differences in age, interests, abilities, and inclinations present challenges to teachers day in and day out. I discussed the first challenge in Chapter 4, and now will address the second—how to engage the different and changing interests of students at various ages in topics that might previously have had no interest to them.

This work of engaging students in topics they were previously unaware of is what the professionals in the school find somewhat familiar, so that part of the challenge need not be seen as unusual. To further mitigate the challenges to be faced, the reasons offered for the value of the chosen WSP will not be lost on students. Most are hungry for ways to belong, ways to matter, ways to connect to one another and to the world. As discussed in Chapter 4, it seems immediately obvious that both the choice and presentation of the topic of study is fundamental to the success of the WSP. Whether determined by local questions or global interests, the subject must be immediately engaging to stakeholders. Also, an attractive description of the proposed final product will add to the enthusiasm of the community at large and of the students in particular. Once the choice of a topic has been made, those responsible for community relations within the school will likely find that this initiative does not vary in any significant respects from other promotional work that they have done.

Still, engaging the imaginations of students in the topic will be one of the daily challenges teachers face, and, while teachers are skilled in doing this, there are special challenges for engaging widely different students and age groups in the WSP. In this chapter I will provide some suggestions about how to engage specific learning toolkits that may be particularly valuable in developing WSPs.

I will suggest some teaching/learning principles that can be used, derived in part from a Vygotsky-oriented exploration of some of the sociocultural tools available to students to make their learning most effective at particular phases of their educational development (Vygotsky, 1962, 1978). That's one way of putting it. Another would be to say that it has focused attention on what students find spontaneously engaging at different ages and then try to infer from their engagement more general principles that can be applied when teaching. Perhaps it will become clear as I give some examples. In giving the examples I will imagine a WSP based on "Castles." I choose this topic because any school anywhere could use it, even though it might have some obvious advantages for those living in an area where there are castles within easy travelling distance. But, like "The Solar System" or any of the other nonlocal topics suggested in Chapter 3, it can be used to illustrate how the learning principles can be brought into play with any topic to engage students at any age without having to rely on the immediate attraction of local relevance. These principles apply to local topics too, but the immediate local relevance will carry one only so far, and these more profound "attractors" will need to be deployed in those cases as well.

My purpose here is not to give descriptions of the teaching approaches that can be found in many good books and websites. Rather I want to focus on approaches that may seem a little unusual at first, but are well suited to WSPs. I will first examine some learning tools that work especially well with elementary school students, then a set that work well with middle school students, and finally a further set best suited to high school students.

LEARNING TOOLS FOR THE FIRST YEARS

The elementary school teacher who is focusing work on the WSP can draw on some of the following learning tools to engage students as they launch into their project. These tools include the story form, binary opposites and mediations, forming images from words, metaphor use, puzzles and mystery, rhyme, rhythm, and pattern, and humor—that is, not the usual array of teaching and learning tools recommended in the average education program or text.

Take the story form. I don't mean fictional stories, though they are hardly excluded. Rather I mean story in the sense that we use the term about the evening news. What's the story on the bridge collapse, or what's the story on the election, on the movie star's latest behavioral extravagance, on the local team's struggle to win the cup, and so on? We are not asking for fictional accounts of these topics. We want the facts, but we want them in a special form, in which the emotional importance of the facts is vividly emphasized, and the facts are organized so that they have the greatest interest and impact. Teachers can invite young students to begin work on their WSP in various subject areas, and can introduce them to it, by asking themselves first, what's the story on it—in the case of the example, what's the story on castles? The idea is to look first for what is emotionally engaging about it, what can capture their imaginations in the topic.

The trick here is to develop a skill all good teachers are expert in: looking at topics in such a way as to engage students' imaginations in their content. They share this skill with the good reporter. "What's the story here?" If the topic is "Castles", the story has to do with the ways in which people have struggled for power and security in particular times and places, how architects have shown great ingenuity, and how those who attacked castles have shown great ingenuity in undermining them (literally), and, gradually, how the security they helped sustain in the end led to their no longer being needed. If that's central to the story, how best to get the young child involved? I will now show how some other learning tools can help.

Binary opposites give the students a first and clear hold on the topic. Bruno Bettelheim (1976) noted the "manner in which [children] can bring some order into [their] world by dividing everything into opposites" (p. 74). Once such oppositions are in place, one can mediate between them and gradually build a more adequate conception, but first one needs to establish some "binary grappling hooks." How can this help younger students orient themselves to engage with, and get their conceptual grappling tools hooked into, the topic of "Castles?" The topic will be introduced by helping students imagine a world where there is much less order, and much less obedience to laws than is common today, which can be done by telling such stories as Robin Hood. In that world of many fewer people, more open spaces, and more wildness, the castle provided a refuge. Many of those who were outside the castles in the area of the Welsh Marches were resentful of the ruling classes of lords, barons, and nobles who were descended from the Normans who had invaded England and even spoke a different language. And even though England had been "pacified" by the Normans, the Welsh were far from content with these invaders pushing into their homelands. The Marches were a frontier, in which the castle dwellers saw themselves as civilized, while those outside the walls were primitive and prone to destructive attacks if given the least opportunity. "Wild lot out there" (often abbreviated to "wild lot") is, in some odd homes, the parting-comment joke from husband or wife as one of them leaves the house for work these days, but in the Marches castles, this was the reality; one didn't go outside the walls without caution and protection, because they were indeed a wild lot out there. So one way to begin to build knowledge of castles is to see them in relation to the opposition of *wild/civilized*. This is far from the whole of the story students will be learning over the 3 years, but it equips the student with a pair of hooks into the meaning of the topic. As they progress, the students will no doubt learn that "wildness" is also connected with freedom, and being "civilized" comes at a price. This is far from the end of the understanding that will be developed over the 3 years, but it is an orientation on which one can build; it is a manner of bringing order into students' understanding of what "castles" can mean.

Images can also help the students engage with "castles," or any other WSP topic. By *images* I don't mean simply pictures, but emotionally charged images that can be formed in students' minds with words. One can have an image of a smell, for example. So I mean something more like an emotionally charged and perhaps diffuse association formed in the mind. The forming of unique images in the mind is one of the great early stimulants of the imagination.

So what emotionally charged images come to mind when one thinks of the wonder of castles? Because pictures of castles are so common today—a Disneyland representation, or horror story pictures of menacing, crumbling castles that are the homes of monsters, or tourist pictures on TV or in newspapers, and so on—these pictures can interfere with students developing richer images of real castles. Many American students at an early age will have seen the old staple Western movies in which the heroes on the frontier are inside the "fort," protected against the threatening natives, who resented encroachment into their traditional lands. They may be taken to see the Alamo in San Antonio, Texas, and try to imagine what that fort was like before a town had grown up around it. The image of a protected place that also includes aggressive extension into hostile territory is a central emotionally charged image that captures something important about the nature and purpose of castles—the original grand forts. Fort simply means a place of strength (from the Latin *fortis*, meaning "strong").

Language Arts classes can be used to tell stories about castles that will evoke images in students' minds. Pictures or TV images, such as in shows like *Merlin*, can actually hinder the development of the skill of image forming, it would seem, and vivid oral stories can better help the process. Initially, folktales about castles may evoke for students the stereotypical pictures they have seen, but as one particularizes the events of the stories that take place in castles, gradually the students' own images will develop, and the emotional associations of those images will stimulate richer meaning. Obviously I am not recommending that teachers not show pictures of the actual castles students will be dealing with, but I am suggesting that a reliance only on such pictures to bring out a deeper level of meaning is not the best idea.

Images in the students' minds will also be stimulated by other accounts of castle life, such as the games children of the time played in castles; the cooking, mending, and clothes making the children would have taken part in; the rhymes and songs sung at the time. These will all help to enrich their senses of what castles were really like. While we tend to think of castles in terms of fortified places of defense that were attacked by those outside, and envision constant violent action, for most of their time they were places where people lived and grew, sowed and harvested food within and outside the castle walls, made clothes, sang and played games, and so on.

As they participate in these stories, rhymes, and games, students can learn words, phrases, and other expressions prominent in castle life: *drawbridge, moat, curtain wall, scullery, keep, tower, ditch, chamber, well,* and so on.

Another of the great learning tools that comes with an oral language is the ability to interpret and generate **metaphors**. This is a capacity of great importance to the elaboration of language. It's a somewhat magical and mysterious ability to see one thing in terms of another. Indeed, sometimes it seems as though we can see almost anything in terms of almost anything else: the tree of life, my heart is a stone, music is the food of love, the foot of the hill. The reader is probably familiar with those exercises that give two random lists of words and invite one to combine any two and explore the new meaning created.

The ability to recognize and generate metaphors seems to be very potent in young children (Gardner & Winner, 1979), tied perhaps to the periods of most rapid language development. We get a hint of this power when we see a 4-year-old playing with an empty box as a house, a car, a shoe, an airplane, all within a 10-minute period. So it will be advantageous to engage this metaphoric ability with the students' WSP topic early on, so they can see it in numerous ways. A castle is literally a defensive/aggressive building, but metaphorically it can be a symbol of idle ambition ("building castles in the sky"), or of immovable power, or of a sense of security in an alien or hostile world (as in the phrase "one's home is one's castle"), of wild ambition—the possibilities are many. Teachers can help the students keep records of metaphoric uses of the topic and explore what these metaphors add to their understanding of it. The story of castles is truly one of strength and security, but many of the common metaphoric uses suggest that strength was always somewhat fragile, or subject to being undermined by a determined and ingenious opponent.

A **sense of mystery** is another tool that comes with language use. Language allows us to describe the world in symbols, and also to lie, to create fictions, and to articulate to others what we know. Mystery is an important tool in developing an engagement with knowledge that is beyond the students' everyday environment. It creates a sense of how much that is fascinating remains to be discovered. All the topics one might select for WSPs have mysteries attached to them, and part of the teacher's job in making any topic engaging to students is to give them an image of richer and deeper understanding to draw their minds into the adventure of learning. Too often teachers represent the world to students as known and represent their task as to accumulate the knowledge that they already have. This is, of course, a part of education, but when teachers forget that their small circle of secure knowledge is bounded by an ocean of mystery, the educational task becomes rather dull. When we make clear that we are all engaged in a journey of discovery, surrounded by mystery, we better represent what the educational task is really like, and open up possibilities and wonder.

If the topic is "Castles," a sense of mystery can be suggested by looking at the silent bare stone remains of castles that once were centers of colorful life and energy. How could those massive expressions of power have been swept away, plundered for their stones, and left to the birds and animals? But standing within the remaining walls, or seeing them in a video, it is easy to feel the faded presence of the ghosts of lords, ladies, lovers, and the workers who made it all possible. It needn't take much to stimulate the sense of mystery. Think how castles have been prominent in the imagination since their real power disappeared, and just mentioning at the right time some mystery connected with a particular castle may capture students' imaginations—an unexplained murder, secret entrances and exits, gardens or moats that have disappeared, hidden passageways exposed by the years.

Rhyme, rhythm, and pattern are potent tools for giving meaningful, memorable, and attractive shape to any topic. Their roles in learning are numerous, and their power to engage the imagination in learning the rhythms and patterns of language—and the underlying emotions that they reflect—is enormous. They are important in learning all the forms of knowledge and experience that are coded into symbols. So the goal will be to find the more vivid and dramatic rhymes, rhythms, and patterns connected with any particular topic. Starting with simple nursery rhymes, suggest young students learn such energetic and memorable rhymes as:

"I'm the King of the Castle
Get down, you dirty rascal!"

One can, with younger students, encourage images of mysterious castle life by drawing on the Little Lost Princess nursery rhyme:

High up on a hill stood a castle of stone
Too tired was the princess to climb all alone
The dove spread her wings and in moments had flown
The little lost princess to the great castle home.

Jokes and humor can expose some of the basic ways in which language works and, at the same time, allow students to play with elements of the WSP topic, and in so doing, discovering some of learning's rewards. This learning tool can also assist the struggle against arteriosclerosis of the imagination as students continue through their schooling—helping to fight against rigid conventional uses of rules and showing students rich dimensions of knowledge and encouraging flexibility of mind. It's always easy to begin with such simple items as:

Q: When is an apple not an apple?
A: When it's a pair [pear].

To "get" the joke one has to be able to see that the same sound often does double duty, and so one begins increasingly to see language as an object and not just as an unreflective behavior. That ability to see language as an object we can reflect on is central to developing what scholars call *metalinguistic awareness*, and that ability in turn is implicated in learning to use language with flexibility and sophistication. So jokes are not just good fun, they are also what Lévi-Strauss (1966) called *bons-à-penser*—good things for thinking with; they have the potential to enlarge our understanding and language fluency.

There are endless castle-oriented jokes, such as:

Q: Who lives in a sand castle?
A: A sandwich

Q: What was Camelot?
A: A place where people parked their camels!

Q: There are many castles in the world, but who is strong enough
    to move one?
A: Any chess player

Q: Who invented King Arthur's round table?
A: Sir Cumference!

Q: When a knight in armor was killed in battle, what sign did they
   put on his grave?
A: Rust in peace!

A servant came running into the king's study. "Your majesty, there's
a ghost in the corridor. What shall I do?" Without looking up from his
work the king replied, "Tell him I can't see him."

* * *

This set of learning tools—the story form; binary opposites and mediations; forming images from words; metaphor use; mystery; rhyme,
rhythm, and pattern; and jokes and humor—can be used to engage the
young students with the WSP topic. This is hardly an exhaustive set, and
no doubt experienced teachers will be able to add a number of their own
that will be at least as effective as some of these. These tools, however,
are helpful reminders that beginning to explore a new topic needn't be
haphazard, leaving students floundering and easily bored. Their interest
in "Castles" or any other topic can be engaged by bringing out the story
about it and thereby showing what is emotionally important about it;
teachers can provide students with grappling tools in the form of binary
opposites; teachers can capture their imaginations with vivid, affectively
charged images; they can encourage flexibility and vividness of understanding by play with metaphors; they can find puzzles in their topic and
surround it with an alluring sense of mystery; and they can enliven their
interest by drawing attention to rhymes, rhythms, patterns, and jokes.

I haven't focused on another commonly used cognitive tool that
develops with language use, and that's the ***puzzle or problem***. This tool
is perhaps too familiar to need much elaboration, but setting up problems or puzzles can stimulate students' explorations in many directions.
The teacher can constantly raise questions that may encourage students
to develop further knowledge: How many different kinds of castle are
there? Which is the biggest and which the smallest? Why are the walls of
castles so thick and so high? What is your favorite castle, and why? How
many people lived in the biggest castle? How many songs and stories
and nursery rhymes mention castles? Why are castles situated where
they are? And so on. See Table 6.1 for a summary of learning tools for
early grades.

Table 6.1. Learning Tools for Grades K–3/4

Some prominent learning tools students from K to grades 3/4 can use in engaging with their WSP

Story	One of the most powerful tools students have for engaging with knowledge. Stories shape the emotional understanding of WSP content. Stories can shape real-world content as well as fictional material.
Binary opposites	Basic and powerful tools for organizing and categorizing knowledge. Such opposites are seen in conflict in nearly all stories, and they are crucial in providing an initial ordering to many complex forms of knowledge.
Images	Generating mental images can be immensely engaging in exploring knowledge. They can attract our emotions and imaginations to aspects of any topic. The use of mental images (as distinct from external pictures) should play a large role in stimulating students' interest in their WSP.
Metaphors	Enable us to see one thing in terms of another. This peculiar ability lies at the heart of human intellectual inventiveness, creativity, and imagination. It is important to help students keep this ability vividly alive by exercising it in learning about and contributing to their project.
Mystery	An important tool in developing engagement with knowledge that is beyond the student's everyday environment. It creates an attractive sense of how much that is fascinating remains to be discovered. All topics have mysteries attached to them, and part of the teacher's job in making exploration of their topics more engaging to students is to give them an image of richer and deeper understanding that is there to draw their minds into the adventure of learning.
Rhyme, rhythm, and pattern	These are potent tools for giving meaningful, memorable, and attractive shape to any content. Their roles in learning are numerous, and their power to engage the imagination in learning the rhythms and patterns of language is enormous.
Jokes and humor	Can expose some of the basic ways in which language works and, at the same time, allow students to play with elements of knowledge, in so doing discovering some of learning's rewards. They can also assist the struggle against arteriosclerosis of the imagination as students continue to learn about and contribute to their WSP.

Table 6.1. Learning Tools for Grades K–3/4 (continued)

Some prominent learning tools students from K to grades 3/4 can use in engaging with their WSP

Puzzles and problems	Pointing out puzzles or problems can stimulate students' explorations in many directions. The teacher can raise questions that encourage students to encounter some attractive difficulty, solving which will enable them to develop further knowledge.

LEARNING TOOLS FOR THE MIDDLE YEARS

Once students become fairly efficiently literate, reading and writing with ease and using many of the above tools in organizing and classifying knowledge, some new cognitive tools come into play. One way to think about the shift to literacy is to see it in terms of a shift from a dominance of the ear to the eye in gathering information (Havelock, 1963, 1986; Innis, 1951; Ong, 1982). Literacy is commonly thought of as a more or less complex skill; but we might better think of it as a toolkit, invented a few thousand years ago, and accessible now to anyone who learns to use those tools appropriately. Literacy brings with it a whole range of additional learning tools that are not commonly thought of when focusing on simply coding and decoding. In this section I will focus on the often-neglected toolkit that comes along with literacy.

Certain activities can facilitate this shift from ear to eye and also show students how literacy can give new powers with the accumulation of new learning tools. Usually these changes begin to come into prominence at about ages 7, 8, or 9. So, the teachers for this age group might be alert to signs of students spontaneously using the kinds of tools described below, and might then help students organize knowledge about the WSP in more efficient and engaging forms.

During these years, the worlds of fantasy fade away and are replaced in some degree by the light of common day, or with what adults recognize simply as a more realistic view of things. Santa and the Tooth Fairy yield to fantasy creatures of a different kind, like Superman, whom students' don't believe are true in the same way, and they yield also to real-world heroes. This new sense of reality does seem to be influenced by particular forms of literacy. As Jerome Bruner (1988) puts it: "literacy comes into its full powers as a goad to the redefinition of reality" (p. 205).

In the kinds of stories that most readily engage students there is a new concern with reality. *Anne of Green Gables* and the rabbits of

Watership Down make quite different accommodations with reality than did Cinderella or Peter Rabbit. Even such fantasies as Superman, Spider-man, and the Hulk and their equivalents all come with elaborate explanations for the fantasy elements of the stories, suggesting that they fit into some kind of reality; fairy godmothers are simply asserted, but Superman needs an explanation, however impossible the account of his escape from exploding Krypton and so on. An oddity of much educational literature at the moment is the suggestion that one can best engage students' interest by starting with what they already know and is a part of their everyday environment. I have earlier suggested why this is odd in the context of what seems to be most interesting to typical students at these ages—those spies, pirates, star warriors, superheroes, the person with the longest fingernails, and so on. (Yes, they "know" some aspects of these—but if this is all the principle is supposed to tell us, it doesn't tell much.)

The everyday world around students is not apparently what they find most interesting; rather, it is the ***extremes of experience*** and the ***limits of reality*** that most powerfully engage students' imaginations as literacy becomes fluent. The reality that is first engaged imaginatively during these years tends to focus on the extremes, on its most exotic and bizarre features, on the most terrible and courageous events—indeed on things that are often most distant from everyday experience. Examples of this kind of material come from sensational newspapers, TV shows, and from publications like *The Guinness Book of Records*. Teachers might sensibly be alert to using this learning tool in expanding students' interest in the WSP into new directions and dimensions. (The attention to the extremes and limits of reality, to the exotic, weird, and bizarre, is not disconnected with students' everyday reality; rather it is how they establish the *context* of their everyday reality and, in some deep sense, its meaning.)

Given the topic of "Castles", students might be encouraged to begin exploring the largest and smallest castles and why they were so different, or discover which was the strangest, tallest, most neglected, had the biggest moat, held out against the longest siege, was overthrown or undermined most quickly, or that was inhabited the longest, and so on. A group of students in a class might start a file on "castle records" to contain such information, soliciting discoveries of extremes or limits from other classes. The exotic and extreme can be routes to massive amounts of engaging information that can be posted online for all other students. And, of course, there are the dungeons, where extremes of experience are only too evident. And there are some castles of astonishing beauty;

some that are rich in amazing stories of heroism, courage, and cunning; some that were governed by the most exotic and colorful characters; and so endlessly on and on.

The Toolkit of Literacy

During the years from around 8 to around 14 or 15, students feel increasing independence, but are typically hemmed in by rules and regulations that they commonly find in some degree at least some of the time irksome. They see much that they want, much that they want to be, and remain relatively powerless to gain either. A learning tool that becomes quite prominent during this period is the *ability to associate with heroic qualities*. We identify as heroes those people who are able to overcome the threats that hem us in, that prevent us from gaining those things we dream of. We lack the money or power or skill to achieve what we would like, so we associate with those who most clearly have the heroic qualities that enable them to achieve precisely what we want. It is a tool that helps us overcome our insecurities; it enables us to overcome some of the threat of alienation involved in the new sense of reality. By associating with those things or people that have heroic qualities we can gain confidence that we too can face and deal with the real world, taking on those qualities with which we associate.

The story of Robin Hood gains a new resonance for students at this age. Now they want to know about the real person behind the story; and what about the Sheriff of Nottingham in his castle? Robin is a mythic figure who reflects the heroic activity of a real person or real people who revolted against the overbearing power and injustices of those who owned the castles. In learning and contributing knowledge to the WSP about castles, teachers can introduce the true stories of the real people who lived and worked and fought inside or outside the castle's walls—in as far as they can be discovered—bringing to the fore the real heroes in these epic stories. Students can associate with the strength and ingenuity of castle defenses and/or associate with the ingenuity and daring of those who fought against enemies within these massive and seemingly impregnable buildings.

Grasping knowledge through human emotions is another effective tool to get beyond the surface of any knowledge to its source in human emotion. All knowledge is human knowledge, discovered or invented as a result of some human emotion. This tool makes it possible to understand knowledge about castles, or any other WSP topic, through the emotions that were involved with their creation or use, and so grasp their deeper human meaning. It is easy to forget that during the ages from about 8 to 15, students make sense of the world largely in personal terms; not personal simply in the sense of their own local interests, but rather in the sense that through understanding knowledge in terms of human feelings comes much of its meaning.

This learning tool also encourages teachers to direct students' attention to the people involved in the story of castles, or whatever the topic. Who were they? What were their motives? Who developed the changing designs of the castles being studied, and against what opposition? In all such cases the question is: What's the story here, or what narrative can be discovered that shows the emotional meaning of the knowledge being learned, and who are the heroes and villains of this story?

The sense of wonder is another key learning tool in our initial explorations of reality. It enables us to focus on any aspect of the world around us, or the world within us, and see its particular uniqueness. It serves like a spotlight, bringing something into bright focus while somewhat suppressing everything else. We can turn this sense of wonder onto anything, recognizing the wonderful in each feature of the world. This tool can provide the gift that makes it possible to recognize something wonderful behind even the most routine and taken-for-granted things. The starting point of all science and all inquiries is "I wonder why. . . ." Wonder provides the ability to imbue any aspect of reality with heightened importance.

The story of castles is replete with wonders—historical, social, technical, aesthetic, strategic, and so on. Groups of students can focus on exploring a variety of wonders about castles in detail, their roles in history and art, developing defensive strategies in changing castle designs, changing strategies for undermining castles by their attackers, the influence of castles on the development of human settlements within and around them, and so on.

Around age 7 or 8, one of the more curious activities of nearly all children begins: They commonly start to collect something or start a hobby. What is going on? Well, one explanation is that they are seeking some security in this new world of reality in which they find themselves; the world might be infinitely extensive and by getting control of some small part of it, through their collection or hobby, they gain some security that it isn't, at least, infinite. These hobbies commonly continue till around age 14 or 15. The learning tool derived from *collections and hobbies* can find energetic work to do in expanding students' engagement with their WSP during this period. One might look for features of castles that open them up to the collecting instinct. All the classes might contribute to the development of a computer database of all the castles in the set being studied; organized according to size, dates, defensive capacities, numbers of people who lived in them at different times, names of known inhabitants with pictures where available, food and water resources, sources of stone for building, current condition with photographs, measurements in all dimensions, games, songs, and stories that would have been common among the children who lived in the castles, and so on. Groups of students can work on tracking down each item and adding information to the accumulating database. Perhaps making a set of "castle cards" would not be quite as attractive as hockey cards to boys, but the challenge of preparing a database, or even a computer tablet app, based on exploring the variety of castles in one's set would likely be engaging to many students.

The kind of intellectual energy spent on students' hobbies and collections can also be harnessed to expand and alter somewhat the work they do in contributing to the WSP. Ideally, some part of the project will become a kind of hobby or collection for many of the students, during the years from around 7 or 8 to 14 or 15.

Changing the context is a tool that enables the imagination to grasp a richer meaning of any topic. The classroom is often an emotionally sterile place—at least with regard to the content of the curriculum, rather than students' own vivid relationships. In general, classroom activities are shaped in significant degree by the context in which they take place, and the daily routines ensure that lessons and units look like one another, resulting in loss of engagement and learning. By shifting the context in which knowledge is learned—often by use of simple devices—students' imaginations can be brought to life, engaging the material much more richly.

As students begin to develop this intermediate toolkit, teachers can deliberately encourage them to take different perspectives on their WSP topic. The goal is to see the topic in many contexts, through many perspectives. If they haven't done so already, a class or group might be encouraged to start looking at castles from the perspective of an itinerant stonemason, or a fruit seller, or cloth merchant, or a local bishop. Or one class or group of students with a teacher might have the task of finding out everything they can about the problems of supplying adequate water to the castle for drinking, hygiene, food preparation, and so on; or how garbage and other waste was dealt with; or where the stone for a particular castle came from and where it went after the decay of the castle. In addition to their usual work on the WSP in different classes—math, science, geography, and so on—all students might be broken into separate groups for one of these "change of context" topics that will encourage a rather different "take" on castles that will be added to the accumulating knowledge base.

Summary of the Toolkit of Literacy

At around age 7 or 8, many students' spontaneous interests change quite significantly, and the kinds of stories and other intellectual engagement they enjoy also change. These changes are clues to some of the new learning tools teachers can deploy to engage their interest in the WSP topic. Improved literacy brings with it a somewhat distinctive conception of the reality the students find themselves in. Their interest in topics can be enlarged by a focus on its extremes and limits, on the strange and exotic, on records associated with it. Knowledge tends to become more engaging if seen in the context of human lives and the human emotions that students share, and especially if they can see new aspects of their topic through the heroic qualities of people involved with it. Teachers will want to draw their attention to the wonderful features of the topic they are learning about—to those things that are attractive because of their unusualness or because they transcend the everyday. Teachers will also seek to show them that their topic has features that can engage the collecting instinct or can be like a hobby. And, teachers will be alert to the fact that changing the context within which they are learning can significantly affect and enliven their engagement in it. These learning tools remain prominent in students' toolkits until around 14 or 15. They don't go away thereafter, of course, but rather they often change as a new toolkit comes into play—that toolkit will be considered in the next section. See Table 6.2 for a summary of learning tools for the middle grades.

LEARNING TOOLS FOR THE FINAL SCHOOL YEARS

By around 15 years of age students who have continued to elaborate the set of learning tools described above commonly experience another quite fundamental shift in their understanding, which can be described in terms of some new learning tools they begin to deploy. The most evident index of this additional toolkit is the use of a new vocabulary in which theoretic abstractions become common. Earlier in their lives, for example, students would have known the meaning of a word like *nature*. They would have thought of it in terms of animals and woodlands, the sea and birds, and so on. What begins to happen at the transition to this new kind of understanding is development of a new meaning to such general ideas as nature so that it is seen increasingly less in terms of sets of particular components and more as a complex system; it is as though the connections between the features of the natural world become more prominent than the individual features themselves. Similarly a whole range of facts and ideas and knowledge take on a new sense and significance by being seen as elements of general *processes* rather than as simply more or less interesting elements.

I hope this isn't too abstract a way of putting it. It's difficult to describe a process of theoretic abstract thinking in concrete terms. Also, I hope it is clear how this new theoretic way of thinking is distinct from the forms of thinking that were shaped by the previous set of learning tools. The shift becomes clear in the way students begin to form theories of history and society, ideologies, metaphysical schemes, and so on. They begin to build a new theoretic world, which they populate with these abstract ideas. One may see this in students who have successfully managed the earlier stages of schooling, and this abstract thinking is less evident in students who have managed less well or who have not taken on much academic equipment during their years of schooling. (This transition is more fully explained in Egan, 2005.)

An example will introduce what I mean. I remember driving our sons to soccer when one was about 13 and the other 16. We were coming up to a federal election, and many of the lawns and windows we passed had sprouted posters in bright red, blue, yellow, and green encouraging us to vote for one or another candidate and party. In the election 4 years earlier, my children had been interested in how many signs were up for "our" candidate, in who had the most signs and the biggest signs, in which party was likely to win, and in how anyone could vote for the villains who opposed our good guys. Putting his soccer boots on in the car, on this later occasion, our older son asked whether we had to pay to have a sign on our lawn, and whether people with the really big signs had to pay more, or did the candidates pay us to put signs on our lawns. I told him that the candidates and their parties paid to have the signs made, or made them themselves, and people put them on their lawns freely to show their support. "But why would people vote for some party because of a sign on a lawn?" he reasonably asked, adding, "Wouldn't people vote based on their principles, rather than be swayed by lawn signs?" We discussed this for a while, and

Table 6.2. Learning Tools in Middle Grades

The sense of reality	The development of rational and logically structured forms of thinking is greatly eased by literacy, and these can be deployed to shape students' engagement in the WSP topic.
The extremes of experience and the limits of reality	Students' imaginations grasp reality readily in terms of its limits and extremes; they focus on the extremes, on the most exotic and bizarre features of reality, on the most terrible and courageous events. These features can be used to stimulate students' engagement with the topic.
Associating with heroes	Enables students to overcome some of the threat of alienation involved in the new sense of reality. By associating with those things or people that have heroic qualities, one gains confidence to face and deal with the real world, taking on those associated qualities. It provides an additional tool to explore human dimensions of WSP topics.
The sense of wonder	This sense of wonder can be applied to anything, recognizing the wonderful in every feature of the world. This tool can provide the gift that allows one to recognize something wonderful behind or in even the most routine and taken-for-granted things. The starting point of all science and all inquiries into any WSP topic can be "I wonder why . . ."
Grasping knowledge through human emotions	Enables one to see beyond the surface of any knowledge to its source in human emotion. All knowledge is human knowledge, discovered or invented as a result of some human emotion. This tools allows one to understand knowledge through the emotions that were involved with its past creation or current use, thereby grasping its deeper human meaning. All WSPs will be amenable to exploring and excavating their core of human meanings and emotions.
Narrative understanding	A narrative context for knowledge can establish its emotional importance while also conveying the knowledge—about any topic. It keeps alive the sense of the "story" the student is investigating.
Collections and hobbies	The drive to exhaustively discover something to give security in a complex world. This tool can be harnessed to allow students to explore aspects of the WSP topic in great detail.

Table 6.2. Learning Tools in Middle Grades (continued)

Changing the context	By shifting the context in which knowledge is learned—by use of often simple devices—students' imaginations can be brought vividly to life, engaging the material in new dimensions.

their questions spread to the ways in which lawn signs were a part of the process of democratic elections.

My point is to give an example of a shift in thinking and in the set of cognitive tools being brought into play. My purpose here isn't to try to explain *why* this change occurs, typically in the midteens among students who have continued to develop the sets of learning tools discussed above, but rather to describe some of its features in a way that illustrates how teachers might engage the *theoretic* imagination in learning. (An attempt at explaining *why* this change occurs can be found in Egan, 1997.)

The Toolkit of Theoretic Thinking

The sense of abstract reality is a tool that develops as a part of the development of rational, logically structured forms of thinking. It has historically been the source of our understanding of the processes by which nature works, and our increasing control over these processes, but can come at the cost of our alienation from the natural world—so that we might see nature, for example, as only a set of resources. In the process of encouraging students' exploration of the WSP, teachers can use, and encourage in students the use of, the abstract language of the theoretical world. Students developing these tools can be encouraged to ask and answer new questions about castles from those being addressed by their younger fellow students. This contribution needs to be valued too. A dictionary of word origins can be invaluable for elaborating on the etymology of theoretic language, and thereby supporting the development of theoretic learning tools.

The more theoretic students could be encouraged to explore other features of castles. They could see them as part of social relationships that necessitate constant concern with security, and so drive and reflect particular world views. What images of the world were held by those most involved in the castle system—both those within and those outside the walls? Or how do castles compare with other defensive systems designed for groups of people—such systems as walls around communities with armed watches (or is the castle simply a more effective development of such a system on a smaller scale?), or building defensive places at the tops of hills to which people could run, or on islands, or . . . well, what can the students come up with? How would humans defend a settlement on a distant planet, and against what?

Such students might also contribute a segment to the WSP's final product on the theory of castles as defensive/aggressive systems. These students might also go further than others in comparing the Marches castles to many other kinds of castle, from the ancient world to the present, including, for example, Japanese castles, Crusaders' castles, Indian Mughal forts/castles, and others they can locate and compare and contrast with the Marches castles of their WSP.

The sense of agency is a cognitive tool that enables us to recognize ourselves as related to the world via complex causal chains and networks, so we can become more realistic in understanding how we may play roles in the real world, and understand ourselves as products of historical and social processes. This realization that our very sense of self is a product of the social and historical conditions that have shaped the world around us is often quite disturbing to students, even while increasing a sense of intellectual potency. Teachers involved in the WSP on castles can look for ways to encourage students to take part in activities that will help stimulate their sense of agency. The goal would be to help students to look outward from their project and see how the knowledge they have been accumulating can be brought to bear in the real world or in their own lives—what can they *do* as a result of their studies?

They may begin a segment of the WSP that focuses on the uses of the Marches castles today. Clearly, in many cases they serve educational purposes for schools and provide a kind of entertainment and aid reflection among tourists. Some castles are well developed in these regards; others are simply decayed remnants largely neglected, smothered in tall grasses and creepers, difficult to access and visited only by the most determined, or ill-informed, tourists. Students can survey and otherwise study what roles the castles play in the consciousness of local populations, of visitors, of schoolchildren who visit them. And they can set up subgroups to explore how adequately the castles serve their avowed purposes, how adequate those purposes are, what other roles castles might serve today, and how they would have to be reconceived and set up to be able to achieve them. What actions could the students take that might influence authorities to deal with one or more or all of the castles in new ways to better achieve educational purposes? Using the Internet, most of these activities can be as well managed by students in Ballarat or Singapore as in Ludlow.

General theories and their anomalies is a tool that enables us to generate abstract ideas about nature, society, history, human psychology, and then recognize their inadequacy and rebuild them into more complex ideas. How does this work? I briefly noted above that a distinctive feature of this new toolkit involves forming theories, and some of these are very general and often simplistic. One finds students quite suddenly sometimes beginning to think about whether the world is getting better or worse within a huge historical time frame. If, for example, the student begins to shape a theory of history that is optimistic, seeing, almost in a Victorian sense, progress in all spheres of life, then there are some facts that will be anomalous to this view; some facts will clearly run counter to it. So the fact of Third World poverty, despite excessive affluence in some parts of the world, is an anomaly to the optimistic general theory. The student's theory need not be disproved by such a fact, though. The student can make the theory more sophisticated or nuanced, claiming that the general progress of the world is not regular, and so incorporate the anomalous facts. It could then be pointed out that those deprived areas become a threat to the "developed world" because of their resentment and armed hostility, and also because poverty breeds diseases that are then transmitted around the globe and threaten massive destruction to all societies. The theory then needs to be made yet more sophisticated to accommodate these further anomalies. And so the process of general schemes being threatened by anomalies and the anomalies forcing the general schemes to become more sophisticated to accommodate them, and so on, is one of the tools energetically at work as students build their theoretic worlds.

Teachers at this stage need to be alert for students beginning to develop the most general theories concerned with castles and their role in history, and use this development in elaborating the project. One realm for rich theory development, continuing with examples from above, is a theory of colonialist expansion and related oppression, such that the castle is seen as the main weapon of the oppressive Norman occupying force in England. If the rulers had not been invaders, and treated as such by a hostile population, castles would not have been necessary. The initial theory, then, is a simplistic colonializing view. But there are anomalies to this theory: In the case of the Marches castles the students have to account for the fact that there were many parts of England in which the Normans ruled successfully without castles. Also, connected with this is the fact that they brought a sophisticated and literate administration of justice to the country that had obvious benefits for many groups in society. This was particularly the case in the time of Henry II and his efficient administrators, such as Geoffrey de Clinton and Ralph Basset, whom the king paid with lands on which they might build castles, as Clinton did in Kenilworth. (The lands, in many places in England, retained the names of these administrators, so Clinton and Basset are still common names in England, and in the United States.)

The students who might be working on the historical background for castle development may well begin with the simple theory of colonialism, but then will have to make it more sophisticated as they discover more about the time, recognizing, for example, that many groups in English society benefited from Norman rule, and the need for the oppressive power of a castle—the "Death Star" of the time, for *Star Wars* fans—was unnecessary in many areas of the kingdom. And so it can go on—the more knowledge generated, the more anomalies to the simple colonialist theory will arise, and the more sophisticated again the theory will have to become to account for the anomalies. The goal in raising anomalies, which may become a significant task for the teacher—but the students' own accumulating knowledge will throw up these anomalies as well—is not to overthrow the students' theories, but rather to make them more and more sophisticated. While the students might begin with idealistic views, the gradual accumulation of anomalies might lead them to conclude that the castle, while a weapon of oppression initially, became a civilizing force and, because of the success of its mission, eventually unnecessary. A kind of material mirror of the way the two distinct languages of oppressors and oppressed gradually merged together, creating a flexible and powerful language which, as the oppressive role of the castles ended, was used by Shakespeare and others to some benefit.

The search for authority and truth is a further tool that takes on a particular shape and importance with the development of abstract theoretic thinking. Because meaning is seen to be derived from general ideas, it becomes vital to determine which ideas are true. An objective, certain, privileged view of reality is sought. Among the historical products of this cognitive tool at work have been dictionaries, encyclopedias, and textbooks—repositories of secured knowledge.

The sense that truth and meaning are to be located first in the general and abstract drives the theoretic thinker constantly, even if subconsciously sometimes, to look for the abstract source in which authority and truth can be located. Again, this is an abstract idea itself, so I will give an example: If the abstract thinker loves singing, it will no longer be sufficient to simply prefer one singer to another. She will draw up criteria for goodness in singers, and compare singers in terms of these criteria. As theoretic thinking becomes more sophisticated, this becomes a tricky business. Maria Callas or Lady Gaga may seem best according to some criteria, but Cecilia Bartoli or Ani DiFranco better according to others. Perhaps one should have different criteria and categories for contraltos and sopranos or for different genres of music? Or if a student begins to think theoretically about something as mundane as shopping, he or she might wonder whether shopping has replaced religion for some people, or whether the economic benefits derived from consumption of certain goods that do little for the lives of many consumers are offset by spiritual desiccation and environmental degradation, or not. He or she will reflect on how to reliably compare such things. What are the benefits to our patterns of shopping compared to the way people in oral cultures gathered what they needed and wanted? How can one find the "true" answers to such questions?

The older students who are building a project on castles may be stimulated—and debate among themselves—whether the castle was really just an oppressive weapon or whether it was the seed of modern civilized society. Of course, by the end of the 3 years, they might see it as both. But that more complex understanding will only come from their attempts to discover which of the more simple views is true.

There are many more particular "truths" that will engage students' attention, inquiry, and problem-solving skills. Where did the food for the castle come from really? Is it possible to locate the stones from castles today in other buildings? Was the demise of castles a matter of their becoming unnecessary or because engineering ingenuity had made them impossible to sustain? Did the culture of castles lead to a more civilized life for English society as a whole? Are there nursery rhymes and stories we tell today that are little changed from those told in castles long ago? Which ones and why?

Metanarrative understanding is a tool that allows us to order particular facts or events into general ideas and form emotional associations with them. We don't just organize facts into theories, but our tendency to shape even our theories into more general metanarratives also shapes our emotional commitments to them. For example, think of the different meanings and emotional associations that emerge when we try to make sense of the destruction of the World Trade Center's twin towers on September 11, 2001, from mainstream American and Middle Eastern Islamic perspectives. In the West, this event fits commonly into a metanarrative in which it can be made sense of only as an evil act of terrorists, in response to which a "war on terrorism" is justified. In a militant Islamic metanarrative, the oppressive Western "devils" were being struck by heroic soldiers of God who sacrificed their lives rather than accept continual oppression and the suppression of their values and way of life. This example illustrates how a metanarrative is not just a logical structuring device but is primarily responsible for orienting emotions to the topic. No one is disputing the central facts or events. It is their meaning that is shaped by the metanarrative an individual is using.

Teachers might be alert to the main metanarratives commonly used in making sense of the WSP topic. "Castles" will be subject to a number of different metanarratives. Students might be encouraged to question whether the castle is a symptom of developing civilization or of the persistence of barbarism. In one metanarrative, the resentful and rebellious outsiders are part of an old and more primitive social order that cannot see how the life promoted by the Normans would be superior. In the other, the Normans and their castles will be seen as a brutal and destructive intrusion into a society that was developing impressively by having melded various traditions into a distinctive new kind of society with its own laws, organization, and practices.

* * *

At around 15 years of age many students involved in the WSP on castles will find that the growing amount of knowledge they accumulate begins to require more complex modes of organizing and also, relatedly, more complex modes of understanding. The new toolkit that students develop in response to the array of knowledge contains prominently such learning tools as I have discussed above, including the sense of abstract reality, the sense of agency, general theories and their anomalies, the search for authority and truth, and metanarratives. These tools are related aspects of the abstract and theoretical world that often begins to be built in the mid- and later teen years. Currently, clear evidence of this theoretic form of thinking is perhaps seen in only a minority of students, but I suspect that is due to the fact that so many students are too little engaged in any area of knowledge to kick this process into action. I hope it will prove much more common if WSPs become more widely implemented. I recognize that this section is more complex and abstract than the earlier sections. The kinds of thinking I have been describing, and the learning tools associated with those forms of thinking, are much less common in current forms of education. (For a more extended exposition of some of these ideas, see Egan, 1997.) See Table 6.3 for a summary of learning tools for the upper grades.

Table 6.3. Learning Tools for Upper Grades

Sense of abstract reality	The development of a theoretic world and organizing tools can be useful in further restructuring portfolios and adding new dimensions of interests and materials.
Sense of agency	Enables the students to extend the materials of their WSPs in the direction of social action and engagement. Their growing expertise can be seen as a source of influence in the everyday world around them.
General theories and their anomalies	This provides a mechanism for continued growth and development of the WSP through elaboration of its undergirding ideas and frameworks of organization.
The search for authority and truth	Provides a goad to making the WSP more reliable.
Metanarratives	Encourage shaping the WSP into an emotionally engaging whole to make it clearly comprehensible and interesting to those who will see the final project.

CONCLUSION

In this chapter I have focused on some principles that might help teachers engage students' imaginations in the WSP topic at different ages. I have chosen a set of strategies that are a little unusual, but no less effective. There are, of course, many other strategies that teachers can draw on to help students build their WSPs. A number of books and websites (e.g., Egan, 1997, 2005; Judson, 2010, 2014; http://ierg.ca; http://ierg.ca/ILP/) can give support to the somewhat new teaching tasks that building a WSP over 3 years calls for.

CHAPTER 7

The Educational Foundations of Whole School Projects

Salmon fry in Westwood School.

I hope that the previous chapters provide an adequate account of WSPs and give good reasons why this form of educational activity should be much more widespread in schools and, indeed, become a regular component of schools' curriculum. That said, it seems appropriate to stand back at this point of the book and consider the educational foundations of WSPs. I will show that this fairly novel pedagogical program that schools may deploy for the benefit of children has sound educational foundations.

What I will not be doing is providing the kind of data that are often and appropriately called for when new programs are recommended. As I mentioned in Chapter 5, I am not providing such data because they do not yet exist, as this proposal is new. After many more WSPs have been implemented, and the kind of evaluative data recommended in

Chapter 4 are gathered, I will supply the data. But, some might ask, "Why shouldn't we wait for those answers before we try it?" Because waiting for such data is an obvious way to ensure that no innovative practices occur in education. We have to try things out first, and evaluate them as we go. And we choose to try them out on the basis of the reasoning that makes them seem likely to do educational good. That is, we have to rely on reason, which is not such a bad basis for choices and decisions in schools. We also, of course, do have the experience of early implementations, such as those discussed in Chapter 3 and others currently getting under way, to help guide our decisions.

I will also try to persuade the reader that asking for the kind of data that typically come from measuring program a with program b in terms of some specified set of learning outcomes is never going to be available with regard to WSPs. They are promoted primarily as new components of the curriculum that are to be accepted or rejected on judgments about whether what they offer contributes to our conception of what it means to be an educated person. WSPs are not being proposed as a better means of achieving some agreed end; rather, they represent a proposal for a somewhat different educational end; they add to our understanding of what it means to be educated. To put it bluntly, WSPs are, as I have already mentioned and will explore in the next chapter, more like a social studies program (though obviously on a different scale) than they are like some new literacy program. In the latter case, we will want data to inform us whether the new program achieves our literacy goals better than other programs. WSPs cannot be tested in competition to other programs with the same aims. In the case of WSPs, we have to assess for ourselves whether a person who has experienced a successful WSP is likely to be a better-educated person. There are no studies to show that social studies is "successful." Successful in what? It is in the curriculum because it is believed that teaching the contents of the social studies curriculum will more likely produce what is considered a better-educated person than if it is not taught. A similar assessment is made with WSPs. We simply have to *think* whether this kind of experience adds something of value to our conception of education. There is no technical help for this most important judgment—it is a judgment based on reasons and values. It is easier to call in the "assessment specialists" to provide technical data and numbers, but they can't help here, and it would be a mistake to think they could.

The reader may be beginning to fear that schizophrenia is invading the text. On the one hand I have suggested all kinds of ways to evaluate

WSPs and on the other I am suggesting that it is inappropriate to ask for those kinds of data as grounds for deciding whether to implement a WSP. The evaluation data discussed in Chapter 5 constitute an attempt to discover whether and to what degree the program can meet its objectives. Remember the point made there that one will not find data that will reveal whether WSPs are an educationally good idea because there are no comparable programs. There can be no comparison between WSPs and other programs' ability to achieve the same educational goals because those goals are unique to WSPs.

Even if empirical research results cannot be expected to address the central question about the value of WSPs, one can look for programs with features similar to WSPs that have been in existence for some years, and tease out from them help in making the decision about whether to go forward with a WSP. To that end I will provide a brief overview of the goals and practices of Project Method approaches to learning and Place-based Educational initiatives in order to highlight the educationally valuable features that WSPs share with these programs, but also the ways WSPs are distinct from them. People who promote Place-based Education nearly always assume that they will be studying the local natural and cultural context of the students. Given that we have included topics like the solar system as suitable for WSPs, it will be obvious that our sense of place is a little more, shall we say, expansive. However, there should be much in the literature on Place-based Education and the Project Method that is comparable to the educational values that WSPs promote, even as I present evidence that WSPs can provide schools with something these other programs cannot. I include these also because when I discuss the WSP idea, some people's initial response, seeking orientation from what they already know, is "How is this like the Project Method?" or "How is this like Place-based learning?"

Well, that's a slightly convoluted and torrid introduction to this chapter. I want to show, first, that the most commonly held general ideas about education today are all compatible with WSPs even though some are perhaps more hospitable than others. WSPs should be recognized as adding something new and valuable to schools' abilities to provide educational experiences to their students that nearly everyone agrees fit well with schools' proper roles. Then I will examine two somewhat related programs to see how much WSPs share some foundational ideas with programs that have proven of value already.

THE ROLES OF SCHOOLS: THE CONTRIBUTIONS OF WSPS

We do a lot of things in schools, so many that it can make one dizzy. The array of schooling activities society has pushed into schools includes a huge range of things related to young people in general—way beyond the purposes initially conceived of at the founding of the public school system. Teachers are expected to be involved with students' health and drug regimens, psychotherapy, sports or band activities that can absorb a significant part of many students' school time and energy, car-wash drives aimed at raising money for athletic or science-fair teams or projects that aid children in impoverished conditions in other countries, rehearsals for musicals and plays that can take students out of regular classes, road safety, and so on, with greater or lesser emphasis depending on school traditions, administration preferences, individual teachers' enthusiasms, and so on. Sometimes quite exotic or eccentric activities occur, and their relationships to education seem somewhat remote. Such activities tend to be casually acceptable within the huge array one can see in schools, suggesting that schools are often only vaguely driven by a clear conception of education that selects, directs, and prioritizes their activities.

Part of the problem is that most people in education have a hard time articulating the concept of education that governs their work, activities, and choices, and determines what is essential for proper education, what is peripheral, and what can actually detract from the process. They might have a neat quote that captures a basic belief about education ("I believe in teaching children, not subjects") or it may be something like the general mission statements that all schools and districts seem to have decided are important to guide them, full of grand gestures, rather vague, and much the same everywhere.

One way to bring order to schools' diverse activities, and to help explain the vagueness and complexity of thinking about schools' activities, is to recognize three distinct powerful ideas that constitute what most people mean by *education*, even if they commonly do not articulate their concept explicitly. I propose that we want schools to do three main things. The oldest idea is society-oriented: preparing students to be productive members of society. Any activities introduced to schools whose purpose is to better prepare students for their future social life—skills that are justified in terms of the jobs they will be able to do as adults, the attitudes and commitments that a generally tolerant and humane social life requires, the basic forms of literacy and numeracy that adequate citizenship calls for, and any sports or computer or driving or behavioral skills that successful social life demands—count as *society-oriented*. The goal of education in this view is to shape individuals to become good citizens competent in a range of appropriate skills and equipped with knowledge relevant for their time and place.

The second idea is called *academic*. This concept is as old as the ancient Greeks. This educational practice is made up of all the things we might do with students that are designed primarily to improve their minds—regardless of social utility. So we teach many things that will be of no practical use but give students a fuller understanding of the realities of the world around them, and inside them. So we attempt to teach all students how to prove that in any right-angled triangle, the area of the square on the hypotenuse is equal to the sum of the area of the squares on the other two sides. Or we teach them that we live on a round planet that spins while it travels in an orbit around the sun (rather than that the sun travels around Earth, which seems much more obvious). Or we try to teach that the plays of Shakespeare and the novels of Jane Austen offer, to those who learn to read them properly, unique and great pleasures. These facts and experiences are of value to the mind building a better picture of our world, even though they have no practical use to nearly all the students who will learn them. In schools we teach many things because knowing them is good for the mind rather than good for social life. The goal of education in this view is to teach those special forms of knowledge that will bring the mind to the fullest understanding of the world and experience.

The third big educational idea, which might be called *individual-developmental*, is about 2 1/2 centuries old and is a product of Enlightenment views about nature. Instead of seeing education in terms of the skills one wants children to acquire to become useful citizens or the knowledge one wants them to learn for the good of their minds, people like Rousseau (1712–1778) (as if there were other people like Rousseau!) thought education should focus on the whole person and recognized that education was not simply something done to children for some supposed future social or intellectual benefit, but that the very experience of being educated should be a central focus. Education is what is done during the process, not simply the end product of a process that might itself be tedious, painful, or Gradgrindish. It is contradictory to think that one might become educated by means of a process that isn't itself constituted by the values we hold to be inherent in education. And one cannot make the experience educational unless one better understands how children learn and develop and what motivates them, and so on. Only by understanding the nature of the child can one educate through a natural process of development to full educated adulthood. The goal of education, in this view, is to achieve a holistic development of the individual to her or his fullest potential.

This is one way of dividing up what constitutes the most common concept of education (for a more detailed analysis, see Egan, 2008). If these three main ideas constitute what most people hold as the process of education, do WSPs contribute something to them? Because if they do, then we can feel some comfort that WSPs are well integrated into the main purposes of schooling and education, and are not some exotic practice off to the side of proper educational activity. That is, though WSPs may be currently unusual in practice, if I can show how they contribute directly to central educational purposes, then unusualness is no reason not to consider how they might be deployed in regular schools to meet legitimate educational purposes.

The fact that there might be incompatibilities among these three big educational ideas, such that each interferes with the achievement of the others (as is argued in Egan, 2008), is irrelevant to establishing that WSPs can contribute to each of the somewhat distinct educational goals.

So, do WSPs contribute to shaping individuals to become good citizens competent in a range of relevant skills and equipped with knowledge appropriate for their time and place, and/or contribute to acquiring those special forms of knowledge that will bring the mind to the fullest understanding of the world and experience, and/or contribute to achieving a holistic development of the individual to her or his fullest potential? Obviously, given the arguments and descriptions of the book so far, I think the answer is a resounding yes.

WSPs contribute to development of good citizenship and equipping students with a range of skills relevant to their future life of work and play in a number of ways. They support students' development of a sense of community and shared responsibility by engaging them in working together on a common project during which they learn the value of others' diverse abilities. The work on a large-scale project both enables them to see how joint action can achieve great ends, and also that they can be part of something of significant scale, and that each of them can take initiatives that, with the help of others, can empower them to change the world for the better. WSPs can make important and somewhat unique contributions to some of the socially oriented goals of schooling. Students who will have completed one or more WSPs successfully will very likely be better prepared to take their places as competent citizens in a democracy.

WSPs also contribute to the acquisition of those special forms of academic knowledge that will bring the mind to the fullest understanding of the world. Students will learn about a specific topic in great detail. They will come into contact with experts on that topic and have to classify and reclassify their accumulating knowledge; that is, they will also learn something about the nature of knowledge and knowledge building that will not necessarily have been a part of their regular schooling. As part of this process they will also be involved in trying to discover something new about their topic, enlarging their sense of exploration of knowledge that is, again, not all that common in everyday schooling. In addition, in a well-organized WSP attention will be given to the general principles recommended in Chapter 6: to engaging students' imaginations and emotions with features of the topic. This richer engagement is one component of developing a fuller understanding of the world and experience. The multidisciplinary and interdisciplinary nature of the work on any topic can contribute to students' recognition of the interconnectedness of the seemingly disparate subject areas of the curriculum, and they will likely come to understand that all subjects provide distinct perspectives, each of which has value in building an image of the whole. That is, WSPs can make a significant contribution to students' academic development.

WSPs also contribute to the holistic development of individual students, encouraging fuller achievement of their potential than would be the case had they not experienced such a program. Although many of the goals of the program are achieved by the whole community working together toward a shared purpose, that shared purpose is achieved only by the efforts of each individual partaking in it. Students learn not only about their topic over the 3 years, but they also learn much about themselves in the context of the diverse interactions with others participating in a large-scale project, with its varied studies, growing sense of achievement, joint work with others, and the celebration and pride in the final achievement. These experiences will likely come with an intensity they have not had before, and will be helpful in the development of their sense of themselves, of their skill base, and their confidence. In particular, the appreciation of how something very large can be achieved will add to their sense of what they are capable of and what they might dare to initiate.

So it seems reasonable to see WSPs as justified by their contributions to all the main purposes of schooling as they are commonly articulated.

In fact, WSPs offer such a rich contribution that the case can be supported that they should become a routine part of schools' curricula. It is hard to imagine a better educational foundation than WSPs' clear contribution to all the main purposes of schooling.

It is hard to read anything about education today without coming across arguments for the necessity of delivering to students "21st-century skills." These skills are assumed to be the best preparation for students to develop in order to deal with the problems they, and the society they are a part of, will likely face in the 21st century. Lists of these skills usually include such things as:

- Critical Thinking and Problem Solving
- Collaboration and Networking Skills
- Agility and Adaptability
- Initiative and Entrepreneurialism
- Effective Oral and Written Communication Skills
- Accessing and Analyzing Information
- Curiosity and Imagination

Source: www.21stcenturyschools.com/What_is_21st_Century_Education.htm

At this point, I hope, no further arguments should be required to show how WSPs contribute to the development of all of this set of skills, with particularly powerful contributions to a number of them. In addition, it might be said that the kind of cooperative engagement that occurs in a sustained and large-scale project, which is unique to WSPs, is a further skill set that will significantly add to students' abilities to deal with the problems and challenges of an increasingly complex world. For the most part, what are called 21st-century skills fit into what I have described above as the society-oriented conception of education; some people's sense of the skills equipment needed for the 21st-century social world leads to their emphasizing this particular set. The fact that they are also emphasized by Herbert Spencer (1966 [1854–1859]) for the new world of the late 19th century will no doubt upset no one, as people who promote them today are often untroubled by either historical knowledge or a sense of irony, and administrators and teachers who are similarly untroubled repeat them, and so they have again become current in educational discourse, articles, books, and policy documents.

It seems clear that WSPs can readily contribute to Common Core State Standards of many kinds. I have selected some more or less at random from the Common Core State Standards Initiative (at www.corestandards.org):

- Ask and answer questions to demonstrate understanding of a text, referring explicitly to the text as the basis for the answers
- Cite specific textual evidence to support analysis of primary and secondary sources
- Analyze the relationship between a primary and secondary source on the same topic
- Follow precisely a multistep procedure when carrying out experiments, taking measurements, or performing technical tasks
- Capitalize appropriate words in titles
- Consult reference materials, including beginning dictionaries, as needed to check and correct spellings
- Use sentence-level context as a clue to the meaning of a word or phrase
- Distinguish the literal and nonliteral meanings of words and phrases in context (e.g., *take steps*)

I could take each of these in turn and indicate ways in which teachers in a WSP use their lessons devoted to the project to fulfill any one of the above, or, from my extensive survey of such standards, others too. What the WSP offers to the Common Core State Standards is not a specific program aimed deliberately at achieving them one by one, but rather WSPs offer a context in which students' learning is invigorated and within which individual standards can be deliberately targeted. Instead of separate and artificial exercises for the attainment of a standard, the WSP provides an engaging context within which each standard can be targeted and attained in a richer and more meaningful way.

ENGAGING IN PROJECTS AND PLACES—EDUCATIONAL RELATIONS

I'll begin with the Project Method and Project-based Learning. Here is how they represent themselves on prominent websites. I have amalgamated a few to provide as simple and clear a statement of common features as possible:

The Project Approach and Project-based Learning are two initiatives that use projects to integrate student learning. Projects are not an "add-on" to regular practice; they frame and contain the curriculum. Project-focused initiatives . . . seek to resolve a variety of educational problems. For example, they share a concern over a fragmented curriculum and an equally fragmented learning experience. They oppose educational experiences that neglect the whole child and fail to develop important lifelong learning practices. They share a desire to educate students to be active participants in a democracy, and fear that traditional methods of teaching fall short of this goal. Traditional classroom learning is also associated with a lack of relevance and low student motivation. Projects are seen to offer a resolution to these educational problems by engaging students in active and meaningful ways.

Projects are considered to be educationally valuable because, among other benefits, they provide cross-curricular learning opportunities and engage the whole child in authentic learning. Students are motivated to learn as they investigate real-world issues and problems in ways that support their unique interests and learning styles. Through individual project work students can develop a positive sense of self-esteem. Shared projects support a sense of pride and identity among students and help build a sense of community. In addition to these benefits, projects are considered to be a best practice for developing what are called 21st-century skills. Through inquiry-based investigations of complex questions, problems, or challenges relevant to students' lives, they develop the ability to think critically, problem-solve, collaborate with others, and communicate effectively. Topics vary, but often connect student interest with the local natural or cultural environment. Teachers can use projects in various ways: "Some teachers use PBL (Project-based Learning) extensively as their primary curriculum organizer and instructional method. Others use PBL occasionally during a school year. Projects vary in length, from several days to several weeks or even a semester" (www. projectapproach.org).

How WSPs Are Like and Unlike the Project Method

I think it will be helpful to summarize each of the main points made here and see how WSPs compare or contrast.

Not an add-on: Project-based approaches see themselves very much as dealing with the regular goals and objectives of the curriculum, but as adding an integrative contribution to students' understanding of the regular curriculum material. They aim to provide a counter to what is represented as the fragmentation of the currently dominant form of curriculum. WSPs share the goal to provide an integrative force to the curriculum, but there are also features of WSPs that are very clear add-ons to the regular practices of schooling today.

Projects tend to work within regular structures, and they commonly last a week or a month, and sometimes, but not usually, as long as a few months or even a year. Scale matters. WSPs are designed to achieve the valuable integrative role that good project work can bring about, but they also aim to do more, and have to be reckoned a distinctive new add-on to regular schooling practices.

Then there is a set of goals for project work that echo what are commonly called 21st-century skills. There are apparent overlaps among these rather general objectives that one sees commonly in curriculum documents, texts, and policy statements today—indeed, it is hard to avoid them. Their ubiquity, vagueness, and generality suggest that not all the people using such terms mean the same things by them. They are also open to the slightly intemperate observation I make above—that they were often more fully articulated by Herbert Spencer in the mid-19th century as important skills required for the new world then dawning. But here is another set taken from www.projectapproach.org about Project Method approaches. Projects aim to:

- make students into active participants in a democracy;
- motivate students by dealing with relevant real-world issues and problems in an authentic way;
- support students' unique interests and learning styles;
- provide inquiry-based learning, critical thinking, active learning, and problem solving; and
- teach collaboration and communication skills.

It is clear that WSPs share a number of these goals, but they are also different in some significant respects, some of which turn on different views of education, in my opinion. For example, the choice of topics for WSPs is not overly concerned with "relevant real-world" issues that tie into students' interests. This doesn't mean WSPs aim to deal with irrelevant, unreal-world issues that ignore students' interests. Rather, the choice of WSP can include local and even urgent topics, but it can also deal with quite different topics. One of the underlying principles of the WSP approach is that one purpose of education is to create interests in things students may have no knowledge about. This is tied to the belief that everything is wonderful, if only one explores it in enough depth, detail, and variety, and a further belief that there are no irrelevant real-world issues.

A number of the other items in the list above, such as active learning, inquiry-based learning, and critical thinking, have come to mean so many things it is hard to be specific about the degrees to which WSPs incorporate such goals, but clearly the kind of active engagement of students in the WSP is akin to what any good project offers. That projects in general explicitly aim to encourage communication and collaborative skills and democratic values means that WSPs share these goals, and, given the much more extensive and intricate structure of the 3-year project, might reasonably be expected to achieve them much better than normally is managed.

Support whole-child and lifelong learning: These terms are similar to some of the other terms used above—so shop-worn over a century of use that their meaning has become varied and vague. But in as far as supporting whole-child learning means not exclusively limiting attention to just a bit of the child—like focusing solely on physical training or job preparation—then WSPs do aim at wide involvement of students' range of capacities—intellectual, emotional, social, kinesthetic, and so on—over the course of the study. I am less confident about lifelong learning, though someone who has had the kind of pleasurable learning experiences that one or more WSPs can provide is likely to find an array of aspects of the world more interesting than someone who hasn't. That seems likely to encourage a generally more inquisitive mind, and so an inclination to want to keep gaining the pleasures of learning.

Positive self-esteem, pride, identity, and sense of community: These again seem to be general goals that projects of all kinds can hope to achieve. The distinctive features of WSPs would seem likely to better achieve these goals proportionate to their greater scale.

Connect students' interests to local natural and cultural environments: This might be better left to the next section, on Place-based Education, as this is one area where these two movements most conspicuously overlap.

Perhaps the most distinctive difference between typical Project Method activities and their set of goals described above is that WSPs are generally concerned with academic goals rather than democratic social skills. This is not to say that WSPs promote antisocial, undemocratic deskilling, but rather that many of the social skills are incidental benefits of this approach—though some are more deliberate, such as the community building, but even that is a means to the primary academic and educational purpose. The primary goal of WSPs is to develop students' understanding and knowledge. To do this, one has to involve the whole child, and one has to encourage critical thinking and problem solving and the other primary purposes of the Project Approach. William H. Kilpatrick's (1918) initial goal to ensure socializing of students to democratic American norms is still attached to the Project Approach. WSPs are designed primarily to achieve other educational goals, even if they do a better job of developing these social skills and attitudes in the process.

In Chapter 8 I will discuss the question of how the Project Method of teaching compared with direct instruction, pointing out that their goals were not the same. Of course, both want students to learn specific content, but if the Project Method is also teaching democratic social attitudes, problem-solving skills, and critical-thinking skills at the same time as instructing in the content, one might reasonably expect direct instruction to manage one part of those diverse aims better. But WSPs are different from the Project Method in seeing these additional goals rather as incidental benefits. The academic focus of WSPs, rather than being on social purposes and learning processes that drive the Project Method, should make WSPs less vulnerable to criticisms such as Chall's (2002) about relative failures to ensure knowledge of the content, though WSPs would also be concerned with a richer understanding.

PLACE-BASED EDUCATION

I will begin with an account from Judson (2010):

> Place is a multidisciplinary concept that is being researched in a
> diversity of fields including sociology, psychology, architecture,
> leisure studies, literary theory, education, geography, philosophy
> and cultural studies. In a general sense, places are . . . meaningful
> contexts of human perception of, and participation in, the world.
> Places are culturally defined, shaped by our experiences and the
> cultural tools we employ to make sense of our experiences. So, as
> we encounter the world around us, observing and participating in

the activities of daily cultural life and as we make sense of our experiences, the spaces where we are, the contexts we find ourselves in, take on . . . interconnected emotional and intellectual dimensions. . . . Sense of place involves, thus, both a personal relationship with one's context as well as a certain depth of knowledge about it. . . . Affective and cognitive dimensions weave together to form a sense of place that involves feeling close to nature and knowing about the soil underfoot, the flora, fauna, sources of water, and rock structures. Sense of place is composed of both emotional connection to nature and knowledge about it.

Moreover, with an emotional connection to one's place, it is much more likely one will protect it, making long-term survival more likely. . . . A personal sense of connection with the natural world [supports] a feeling of being "at home" that supports psychological wellbeing. . . . We see, thus, in Ecological Education literature, an understanding of the value of place not only for the knowledge one gains of context but, perhaps more importantly, for the emotional bond that can form. It is this emotional bond that may inspire people to live sustainably. (pp. 73–74)

Judson also notes that Place-based Education differs from conventional text and classroom-based education in that it understands students' local community as one of the primary resources for learning. Thus, Place-based Education promotes learning that is rooted in what is local—the unique history, environment, culture, economy, literature, and art of a particular place; that is, in students' own *place* or immediate schoolyard, neighborhood, town, or community. In the view of many Place-based educators, grade-school students often lose their sense of place through focusing too quickly or exclusively on national or global issues. This is not to say that international and domestic issues are peripheral to Place-based Education, but that students should first have a grounding in the history, culture, and ecology of their surrounding environment before moving on to broader subjects.

Central principles of Place-based Education include immersing students in local heritage, cultures, landscapes, opportunities and experiences; using these as a foundation for the study of language arts, mathematics, social studies, science, and other subjects across the curriculum; and emphasizing learning through participation in service projects for the school and/or local community (www.promiseofplace.org; www.bie.org/about/what_is_pbl/).

How WSPs Are Like and Unlike Place-based Education

Place-based Education is, in one obvious sense, more focused than Project Method approaches, even though the focus on local cultural and physical environments is one that is also prominent in many school projects. While building an understanding of the "soil underfoot" and the cultural and natural surroundings of the student can also be the goal for many projects, they are the consistent focus of Place-based programs and, indeed, their *raison d'être*.

WSPs are both like and unlike Place-based Education in that they share the goal of immersing students in knowledge and are long-term commitments, while second, WSPs may engage with topics that are unrelated to the local environment and the soil underfoot. Also, Place-based Education is not time-limited in the way a WSP is, and might be seen as a somewhat distinctive approach to pedagogy in general. The WSP's "sense of an ending" contributes a deliberate end point and product for the project, different from Place-based Education.

In general, Place-based Education is distinguished by its local emphasis. Certainly WSPs offer related locally oriented learning experiences, as is demonstrated by all three examples—one of which explicitly associates itself as using principles of Place-based learning as well. But one could easily imagine a school in which one, two, or three teachers took a Place-based approach to their teaching while the rest of the school went on as usual. This couldn't happen with a WSP approach, where the schoolwide topic provides a specific, unifying focus.

WHY DO WE NEED WSPS?
WHAT JUSTIFIES THIS EDUCATIONAL PROGRAM?

The Project Method or theme-based learning, and Place-based Education are responses to the shortcomings of a traditional approach to schooling that segments the curriculum, diffuses learning, and where classroom routines create a generally dulling uniformity to students' school experience. The WSP approach actually takes the notion of an integrating project to a level that has real impact on the problem—weekly or monthly themes/projects in classes do not necessarily provide enough context or content for students to understand the integrated nature of the world the topic focuses on.

WSPs offer educational benefits that are different from those offered by traditional forms of schooling and also by Project approaches
or Place-based Education. WSPs have the specific goal of being primarily
intellectually rigorous and exploratory academic programs that ensure
significant extensive and intensive knowledge of their topics; they are
truly long-term, creating possibilities for deeper understanding and personal commitment to a common enterprise in ways rarely achieved in
schools. The area where they do have a social purpose is in the building
of a vivid sense of community, but this comes as an incidental product of
the serious engagement with learning about the chosen topic and jointly
working toward a specific product that will celebrate its conclusion.

Theoretically WSPs have a somewhat different end in view from
other like-sounding programs, though there are educationally worthwhile areas where they overlap. WSPs can invigorate learning by
providing students with firsthand experiences that deepen their understanding of the interconnected nature of knowledge of the world.
Practically, we see that WSPs provide, among other benefits, a shared
purpose for staff and students alike that over the 3-year span of the program can lead to community building and identity creation unmatched
by other programs.

CHAPTER 8

Whole School Projects: Objections and Responses

A display of indigenous plants.

Rather than simply list questions and answers here, I'll add a (very) small element of drama by suggesting that a proponent of WSPs has made a presentation—a kind of condensed version of the previous chapters—to the senior staff of two large schools, one primary and the other a nearby middle school, where most of the primary school students go. The principals, vice principals, and department heads have previously indicated willingness to consider jointly taking on a WSP in their schools, which will involve an unprecedented degree of cooperation among them. Not that there has been any lack of coop-eration; they share certain social problems that have formed the basis of joint meetings of the staff of both schools, and the fact that one is a feeder school to the other has also required cooperation of various kinds. But they have never contemplated cooperation on an academic project of this scale. In such circumstances sensible people first look for reasons why not to start such a project. And, just to make it more realistic, a number of the administrators see the possibility of such in-terschool cooperation as a bridge too far, but do have some interest in possibly adopting a WSP for their own school.

They have listened to the presentation with varying degrees of interest and skepticism, and have questions they want to ask before moving to a discussion among themselves about whether to take on a WSP. Assume that their schools are in a suburban area. Neither of the schools is a high performer in the region, and teachers tend not to stay for extended periods of time, with good younger teachers in particular constantly looking for better schools to work in. These problems, and recent poor assessment results, have persuaded a number of the senior staff to look for something other than routine school improvement programs—which haven't worked well for them in the past—and so they have consented to hearing from a Whole School Projects team member, hoping a WSP will help build community and invigorate learning.

Like nearly all educational administrators and teachers, they are eager to find new ideas that will help them improve their practice, but they are also wary and knowledgeable about generations of supposed "great new programs" that have quickly failed to deliver on their prom-ises. Indeed they are wary in large part because they are "innovation-exhausted," constantly being pushed by senior administrators and state and federal officials to adopt a new program that will work educational wonders, but never does. And here comes another. True, WSPs do look quite different from the usual array of 'innovations," some of which are innovative only in name, with the program only cosmetically different from many failed "innovative" programs lying in the educational dust.

To make the scenario more vivid, I have created sketchy characters for the questioners, in order to better understand where the doubt is coming from. Each Q question will be followed by an R response. One of the questions is transcribed as accurately as I can recall from an ac-tual discussion. (No prizes for guessing which question.)

Q 1: It's just too complicated.

[A science teacher in the middle school. He has been with the school for 12 years.]

One obvious reason this is going nowhere is the scale of organization needed to make it happen. Maybe a few private schools with big budgets have the additional staff something on this scale would need. You'd have a really big job just coordinating all the groups, all the different classes, let alone have our two schools work together, all dealing with a single topic. But pressures on regular schools make it quite simply impossible, regardless of what you said earlier about regular schools being able to implement such whole school projects. Assessment pressures, other programs, and we just have to spend a lot of resources on raising literacy scores—so many problems I get tired just trying to list them—don't leave us with the administrative resources for this, not to mention the financial resources. I wonder if you have any idea what we're up against that makes WSPs just out of galaxy for us?

R 1: It's just too complicated.

Doing anything new and different always seems bigger at the front end than looking back when under way or when finished. It is unquestionable that WSPs are not going to get under way casually or without major commitment by the whole school and a commitment of resources by the administration. I guess the first thing I'd ask you to consider is that schools—as you well know—do lots of things. Not all of those things are equally valuable educationally. WSPs offer something that you might be willing to agree can be educationally valuable, even though you think it's a value beyond your schools' achieving, due to lack of resources. But I wonder if that's really true. You admit that you are under the assessment gun because of inadequate achievement levels, yet you seem to think you have no alternatives apart from more of the same kinds of programs that are not obviously getting you further ahead.

Well, I would add that I sympathize with your situation and the difficult problems you face. But I want to argue that beginning a WSP is not a total change of curriculum for you—it's maybe a couple of classes a week, or more or less some weeks, and maybe some other activities, all of which will need initial coordination, but which, once under way, can go surprisingly easily, with the teachers and their classes taking much of the initiative to keep the project growing.

Also—and this is my main point—there are reasons to expect that the WSP might prove to be a better route to achieving the objectives you currently think prevent you from trying it. Does that need unwrapping? I want to emphasize my earlier point: The objective to drive up basic assessment scores has you tied into certain practices you think are the only direct ways to achieve that objective and so you can't take on a WSP, but you may find that a WSP is a much more effective tool to achieving improved scores, because you will have a more energized teaching staff and motivated students whose learning is invigorated.

There are a number of schools close to the Columbia River Gorge, and nearly all those students travel through and across the Gorge. But those to whom it has increasingly become an object of wonder are those who have been studying it for years as a WSP. If you care to look at what has happened to the achievement rates of the children in that school, you might be surprised (as I mentioned earlier, at the time of this writing Corbett Charter School in Oregon is the #3 school in the United States according to the *Washington Post*'s Challenge Index ranking of 1,900 schools nationwide; see Chapter 3). It would be wrong to suggest that this is due simply to the WSP, of course, but the project is clearly a crucial element in stimulating those children's engagement in their work across the curriculum—because all curriculum areas contribute to the students' knowledge about the Gorge. (It should also be noted that Corbett Charter School is a public school, is funded at a level that is below the state average, and faces all of the requirements of No Child Left Behind. The administration and teachers in the school have learned to reject conventional [even National Conventional] wisdom regarding meeting grade-level benchmarks. Their strategy is explicit. They meet every standard at every grade level on the way to doing something really interesting.)

Those students who struggle to find adequate reasons to become literate and numerate may find themselves using these skills in a context of clear meaningfulness. Easy to be idealistic in the abstract, but maybe too easy also to find reasons not to try an unfamiliar route to the old objectives. Perhaps I can encourage you at least to keep open to the possibility that the WSP may help you to achieve what is currently so difficult, and it might also achieve other educational benefits as well. The invigoration promised is not only to the students' learning but is also to the whole school community as it engages on such a common project.

That implementing a WSP is financially doable is beyond question, because it is being done, in a way that puts no great strains on budgets. It requires leadership and, among the teaching staff, something more than an attitude of simply going along—that is, it does require preparation of a kind that builds some enthusiasm. But it is not as costly as you might imagine (as you can see from the examples in Chapter 3)—so that reason for not launching into this new galaxy, as you put it, can be laid aside. Remember, too, that the organizational problems need not be as alarming as maybe they might appear initially—especially if you deploy an overall plan, decentralized control, distributed problem solving, involve multiple interactions, and adaptive behavior.

Q 2: The topics are too academic, and no topic will capture everyone's interest.

[Principal of the primary school, whose background is in early childhood education. She is dedicated to Progressivist ideas and practices, encouraging her teachers to start always with students' experience as the first building block for any new subject.]

The WSP seems to me to have real possibilities, even though I do agree with my colleague that the planning of the project presents challenges. My concern with the description so far concerns what seems to me a too academic focus. I think we might manage such a project far better if we were more attentive to the environment and needs of the children. I mean, why the artificiality of planning some specific product based on "insects of the desert" or whatever? Even when focusing on some local feature, you want to turn it into an academic program rather than let the students' interests determine what they want to explore. And none of the topics you mention is going to engage everyone's enthusiasm. You need to attend more to the interests of the students in deciding the topic, and I would focus more on the social learning and the social utility of the project than the academic focus you have been proposing.

R 2: The topics are too academic, and no topic will capture everyone's interest.

I suppose those of us promoting WSPs begin with the belief that everything in the world is wonderful—that is, full of wonder—and the more one knows about anything, the more it discloses its wonders. The problem with so much of schooling, as everyone seems to be aware, is that we have created a curriculum that includes so much that we are constantly moving students through it, trying to ensure coverage and having too little time to explore anything in depth. It's the problem usually described as having educational curricula that are "a mile wide and an inch deep." Only when we can pause and explore something in depth do its wonders emerge (Egan, 2011). Again, the examples of Qingdao, Westwood, and Corbett schools show that the academic study of their topics do not make them any less exciting for the students; indeed, they recognize that this is no trivial or trivialized exploration they are involved with, and their contributions are meaty and significant. *Academic* shouldn't be a term of disparagement for educational institutions! It is centrally what they are about.

As I noted already, the business of educating children crucially involves engaging their interest in new things. Some educators still assume that engaging students' interest in new topics happens only by starting with what they know and gradually expanding from there, but such a belief is unhelpfully restrictive (Egan, 2002)—that is, the "only" part of it is false. We do, of course, need to select topics that we know have the potential to interest everyone if they are explored appropriately. If the topic is important, then it is our educational duty to find a way to present it to students in as engaging a manner as we can. So I don't think it is educationally important to let students' current interests drive either the choice of the topic or the dimensions to be explored. In the beginning they will know little or nothing about it, and the teachers will know more. As time goes by, of course, students' developing knowledge will give them good grounds to suggest directions and approaches for continuing work. I am aware that this fringes an issue that has become embroiled in ideological conflicts, but I think this response is a matter of simple common sense.

I also think that the social values of the learning environments and activities will inevitably follow their academic purposes, and need not be seen as somehow separate.

In most cases, I think that gaining general acceptance for the topic, provided it fits the criteria mentioned earlier, will not be as hard as might be expected. Much depends on choosing the topic well and describing it in a way that captures its most engaging qualities. So, education is about creating interests, engaging imaginations and emotions, and not simply responding to those already established or always beginning from them. "What's Hecuba to him, or he to Hecuba, that he should weep for her?"

Q 3: Impossible because of other curriculum demands.

[Head of the math department in the middle school. He has been in the school for only 2 years and is ambitious and eager to improve the math achievement levels in the school.]

The amount of curriculum time we are given to meet Common Core State Standards and expectations in math is already squeezed to the bone. Covering the curriculum if you have a class of gifted students is one thing, but meeting the requirements with a mixed ability group, in which we have a high proportion performing below grade level, is tough. We have just undertaken a new reorganization of the curriculum, and all our teachers have taken extensive professional development workshops in new teaching methods, and we are set to turn our achievement levels around.

What I am describing for my department is true in one way or another for every other department in the school. I can see that math can be tailored to the WSP—that is, I can fit it to some part of the project without much strain. And I can see that this real-world use of math might even make it more interesting and meaningful for the students, but this will take time and effort that I'm not sure I can give. And while I can see how this *might* be possible for me, I'm not at all sure how my colleague teaching about, say, the French Revolution, is going to fit her teaching to "insects of the desert," or whatever. I mean, we've got a really tight curriculum to cover and this is asking us to add to our workload for planning and even lose some curriculum time, certainly in some subjects more than others, for meeting our regular mandated objectives.

R 3: Impossible because of other curriculum demands.

I recognize that it is hard to imagine integrating such a large-scale program into regular schedules and teaching activities without taking a huge amount of time and effort, all in addition to the pressures that drive most teachers. I have two general responses. First, when we talk of WSPs "invigorating learning" we mean the teachers' learning no less than the students'. WSPs give energy to those who launch into them. The developing end product allows teachers to see a tangible expression of learning in a way usually not easy to see in the routines of covering parts of the curriculum, and even less easy to see when the only product one gets is test scores. Energy and engagement do not create extra time, of course, but they do allow us to use the time we have more effectively. So I think this increased engagement and effectiveness in learning will reduce the impact of this entirely reasonable objection.

Second, I really don't think it will be as hard to incorporate the WSP into nearly all areas of the curriculum as it may seem initially. Granted, if a teacher is teaching the French Revolution, then the "flora and fauna of the desert" is hardly an easy match, and the history curriculum in general (unless the topic is something like castles or something that fairly easily fits in with the regular history curriculum) might be pushed to find connections to the topic in the regular course of teaching. I'll come back to the history curriculum, but for most other curricula subjects it should not require much ingenuity to find ways in which connections can be made to the topic, especially if the topic is chosen with the array of curricula objectives in mind. I will add that the topic will run 3 years, and during that period teachers of math or art might become intensely involved for some part of the time, because it will be easy to connect their curriculum content or activities to the topic; and at other times they may be less involved. Math, science, social studies, art, and so on will all have significant features of their mandated curriculum and skills objectives that can be met within the WSP, even though most of their curricula work will go on quite separately from the WSP—it isn't designed to be all-absorbing of time, just absorbing for some of the time for all students, teachers, and administrators.

History, however, does present distinct challenges. One obvious solution would be for the history department to find some time during the year to look at historical dimensions of the WSP, even if that is quite distinct from their curriculum objectives. It can always contribute something toward students' development of historical methodology, of course, but I acknowledge that it might prove difficult for some teachers and their classes to make major contributions to the developing product of the WSP. Even so, those students will be contributing through their other classes. But this is an objection to which I cannot offer a satisfactory response.

When it comes to most curriculum areas, however, I am not convinced by the image of a crammed curriculum with not a minute to spare for planning related to the topic of the WSP. In math, for example, it should be easy to find things in the project to measure and count and graph and calculate and analyze, and use whatever math skills are mandated. If we were to take as an example the topic of "flora and fauna of the desert" one can see fairly easily how art and geography and biology and science and nearly all other subjects can become involved. And, again, care in the choice of the topic can minimize the impact of this objection of mandated curricula objectives preventing the WSP going forward. Also, every topic chosen will give opportunities that are easy for some curriculum areas and less for others. If the historians are somewhat neglected with one WSP, they might be given an inside track on selection of a subsequent WSP.

Q 4: It will be too costly.

[The deputy principal of the middle school. She has been in her
current role for 4 years, had previously been a science teacher for 2
years, and throughout her 6 years in the school has coached the girls'
field hockey team. She has a major responsibility for the budget.]

I am concerned mainly about the added cost of such a project
to the school. You can't expect such a project to be organized without seconding some staff members to be on the organizing committee you mention. Even if that is just relief from some classes, we will
have to pay for substitute teachers, and management of the project
will continue to be a cost for the full 3 years of the project and even
through the 4th year where the earlier work is to be presented, developed, and exploited in various ways. You have casually mentioned
the product, and given an example of the mural in one school, which
will have generated a significant cost, having artists produce the basic background representation. You have mentioned fieldtrips to some
sites, when that's possible and appropriate—not to the outer planets, I
hope. (Some laughter.) And there will be materials of various kinds. I
think this—which is an add-on to our regular curriculum—will make
a major hit on our budget.

R 4: It will be too costly.

Yes, planning and running a WSP will cost. And, during times when
schools' budgets are under pressure anyway, the idea of taking on a
wholly new and large-scale program like this will not immediately appeal to those who are responsible for the school's finances. My main
response to this concern is just a variant of one I have made already
to other objections: Schools do many things, and not all of them are
of equal educational value. A well-chosen and organized WSP can add
considerable educational value and might reasonably be the beneficiary
of some less educationally effective program having its finances reduced.

But, having said something so provocative—because all those other
programs will have energetic proponents, so it is not likely that reassign-
ment of finances can be counted on to be uncontentious—it is important to emphasize that WSPs do not necessarily cost much at all. The
large-scale redirection of energies and the construction of some major
new product may make it seem as though the WSP must be expensive,
but this is far from being necessarily so. In some cases, the WSP can

benefit from some small-scale redirecting of activities: The fieldtrips that are not an uncommon feature of schools' activities and a call on budgets can in some cases be redirected to the WSP. The cost of a trip around the moons of Saturn might strain most schools' fieldtrip budget, but more appropriate trips related to the WSP need not add much. The main evident cost will be in buying time for the organizers of the project. In many cases—certainly in the case of the examples you have read about earlier—much of that work was done on a voluntary basis, and so cost very little, and in all three cases the relatively small costs were mostly absorbed without any evident strain on school finances. While the WSP is a big item in the life of the school and the educational experience of students, teachers, and administrators, it need not be a big-ticket item.

Also, while there is no necessity of a WSP being expensive when compared to other program costs, it is precisely the sort of activity that can attract donations from the community and win subject-specific grants. The potential for gaining grants-in-aid might be a criterion for selection of a WSP focus. Such grants can buy the time of the organizers of the WSP and/or fund a part-time coordinator for the program. Of course, one can't count on such funding, and even searching for it will take time and energy, but grants and other gifts, of volunteers' time and energy, are often easier to attain than some might assume. Retired grandparents with a willingness to volunteer time, energy, and skills to their grandchildren's school can be a significant resource that can support such a project.

Q 5: How will you assess it?

[District learning specialist. She has been in the position for 8 years, and had previously been a high school social studies teacher for 11 years before doing a PhD in educational psychology.]

What kind of indicators will suggest to you that the WSP is going well? Doing what it should? Achieving all those objectives you mention? And how will you know if it was doing poorly or being generally inadequate? How will you know if some units are doing well for the project and others are not contributing adequately? In short, how do you plan to assess the WSP?

R 5: How will you assess it?

The WSP will have a number of purposes, so many forms of assessment/evaluation will be appropriate. One role of the organizing committee, as I mentioned in Chapter 7, will be to lay out a plan for achieving the objectives, with markers for each major stage to be achieved by the various component groups as they work in the direction of the end product. The groups themselves—usually class groupings—can help articulate these markers as they begin work on the project, revising them as they become more expert in understanding what they can reasonably hope to achieve. So, like the bees and ants, they will constantly monitor how adequately they are meeting the stages of the plan and rearticulate those stages and the markers as they go forward. So this will be one of the main tools of assessment, and will be a significant part of the job of the continuing supervisory committee. But, again, this has to be a flexible process. If groups become obsessed with reaching goals provisionally described before the project was under way, especially if it becomes clear that some of those goals were either unrealistic or not the best way to go, or too modest, or whatever, then they need to be rearticulated, with new assessment markers described in appropriate detail. Such changes will need to be coordinated with other groups, of course.

Smaller-scale assessments will need to be conducted, and these will vary depending on the particular tasks to be performed by groups within the overall project. So, if one subgroup is working on a multimedia presentation based on the group's work, or if one or two members from each group are given responsibility for making and upgrading a webpage for the project—which can itself become a tool of assessment—or those doing artwork, or perhaps writing a song about the project, or those who might be producing a traditional written or word-processed paper or writing up results of fieldtrips, and so on, will properly need to be assessed in different ways. Assessment strategies can include performance of tasks to specified standards, teacher observations of the group's contributions, or standardized testing related to elements of the WSP that coincide with mandated requirements in some particular curriculum area.

A significant part of the assessment of WSPs will be from students and teachers developing evaluation rubrics with clear markers of achievements or performance indicators. A rubric simply lists criteria that indicate the important components of the work being assessed. The criterion is articulated in terms of different levels of completion or competence, with a weighted score assigned to each level 1 to 10, or A to D-. An adequate rubric gives clear guidelines to others on how to assess work that contributes to the project. As the criteria for assessment will be clearly defined, different assessors will arrive at similar conclusions when comparing a group's work to each of the graduated criteria on the rubric.

The question of how one might assess whether the WSP is a success can again be managed in terms of clearly specified objectives for the project and how adequately they are met—even though the objectives might be adjusted in response to circumstances and increased expertise as the process goes forward.

However, it is likely that the main assessment criterion for most people involved in a WSP is just a sense of how it is going generally, judged by the buzz it creates in the school and the quiet satisfaction people feel as they work.

Q 6: Too many programs.

[Cross-grade elementary school teacher, with a special interest in critical thinking and multiple intelligences.]

Your group also proposed another novel program you called Learning in Depth, which I've heard people talk about as LiD. In that program you suggest that each child, near the beginning of their school career ideally—though you do acknowledge it can begin at any age—should be allotted a topic, such as birds, the circus, apples, railroads, and so on, and then build a portfolio on that topic over the following years of schooling. For most children, that will mean they will be building their portfolios over 12 years or so, to make each child an expert on their topic. Regardless of how educationally sensible or otherwise this idea is, the question here is how are these two programs are supposed to be coordinated or related? I mean, are the topics of the LiD program supposed to match features of the WSP topic? And how is a school supposed to deal with both these additional projects, when schools are already over-burdened?

R 6: Too many programs.

The two programs are quite separate and should not be seen as in need of any relating or coordination with each other. They can continue working in a school quite independently, and the students can be involved in both programs without any concern that they either support or interfere with each other. They do have in common the fact that they have been designed to provide educational experiences that schools currently inadequately provide, and often do not provide at all. They offer students important educational experiences, enabling students to add significant new dimensions to their learning. Also, the programs do not rely on each other in any way, so it would be entirely possible to implement one without the other.

The issue about how any school might be able to implement both these programs is not really my concern here, but I can see no reason why both can't be working in the same institution (as indeed they are in two of the three schools described in Chapter 3). Also, LiD does not require the concerted organization that the WSP requires; LiD can carry on in the background, as it were. No doubt the WSP will provide some material for some students' LiD portfolios, but that's not a necessary or planned feature of either program. LiD is an individual program—each student having a different topic—and WSPs are joint efforts with children working together toward the same end product.

Q 7: Moves toward uniformity and away from individual approaches.

[A teacher in the primary school. She has been in the school for 8 years and is committed to individualizing instruction as far as possible, and in pursuing "personalized learning" programs.]

I have doubts about any approach in which everyone is studying the same thing. Any program that does this tends, at least, to reduce opportunities for students to follow their own individual modes of learning and interests. This seems especially the case when everyone is supposed to be working toward the same goal at the end, reducing further the possibilities for individual flair and styles; everyone is constrained by adding pieces to some predetermined whole. In my school we have been working toward a personalized learning approach that ensures each child's individuality is put front and center of all our learning activities. A WSP would seem likely to undo that work and move us in the opposite direction.

R 7: Moves toward uniformity and away from individual approaches.

First, it should be remembered that any WSP will consume only a relatively small amount of time for any individual class. Each week, maybe one or two classes might be devoted to some aspect of the project along with the occasional fieldtrip, so it is not as though the WSP will displace all other activities in the school or for any individual student. Second, the fact that there is a single product aimed for does not mean that there will not be significant opportunities for diverse contributions being made to it. Classes will take on particular foci, and individual students can contribute in distinctive ways to the class focus. That is a matter for how the individual teachers and organizers of the WSP set about it. The work you have done toward individualizing your instruction and students' learning need not be negatively impacted by the WSP. The fact that all the students have to learn Pythagoras's theorem or about the food groups does not undermine possibilities for individualizing learning.

Q 8: The requirement of a specific product.

[A school board member, who has heard about the presentation on WSPs and is initially attracted by some of its features. She is prominent as a promoter of education in the community and is the CEO of a locally based international transportation company.]

Surely your notion of a "product" at the end might give pause to some who might otherwise embrace a schoolwide project. It seems that a product or presentation might very naturally arise out of this sort of work, but it seems unwise to try to describe the final product in detail upfront—even if you plan to be flexible about the specifications of the product in the light of experience. It might simply feel too daunting if the requirement to put together some big production at the end is seen as something "in-addition-to" the rest of the work.

R 8: The requirement of a specific product.

The final product is important in both providing a sense of direction for the WSP and to provide everyone involved with markers and specific objectives on the way. Also, the final product contributes a great deal to many of the objectives of the WSP program—such as the sense of pride, the sense of how something very large can be achieved by many small contributions, and so on. There are many educational purposes built into the WSP idea that can be achieved best only if there is some specific product plan guiding the whole process.

As I have noted a few times, the WSP needs to maintain flexibility throughout, but it does need to have a clear end product, even if that clear sense of the end product has to go through some changes. For example, imagine a common kind of project one might find in schools today, such as reclamation of a pond. In a WSP, which will be on a larger scale than the project one might find today, the 1st year may be given over to all classes spending time studying the life and threats to the life of the pond, and to other ponds in other places and conditions, creating understanding of what conditions are necessary for a healthy pond. While a reclaimed pond remains the final product, what will need to be done to achieve that will only gradually emerge during that 1st year. And then, of course, conditions might be such that significant problems arise for our hope to reclaim the pond in the time we have available. A road might be built through the area, a housing development might swallow it up, or some toxic accident might make the originally planned final product impossible to achieve. So the final product may change, and you may set about creating a pond somewhere else, or reclaiming a different pond. But without that imagine of a final product, simply learning more and more about a particular pond or ponds in general will lack the kind of direction and urgency that having a final product in mind can provide.

Q 9: This is just a version of a common educational practice, and a rather eccentric version at that.

[A computing science teacher in the middle school, he has been there for 6 years and tries to integrate his specialty with that of other teachers in the school.]

You are suggesting this as some kind of new program, but there have been endless versions of this idea around. At the moment lots of schools embrace a "theme"—such as your example of reclaiming a pond—for a year or more at a time. I don't see how this is any different, except that it goes on longer—which itself doesn't seem to be a necessary advantage because it introduces all kinds of additional problems for schools' organization. Also, you want to include everyone in the school, whereas most current projects only involve a single class. What you are proposing is a common practice except that what is distinctive about your proposal simply introduces a bunch of additional requirements that make it unworkable.

R 9: This is just a version of a common educational practice, and a rather eccentric one.

Well, I have throughout acknowledged that this is hardly a new program, in that there are, as you note, practices somewhat like it evident in many schools. Perhaps calling it a "common" practice rather overstates matters, unless you want to include all small projects that are somewhat out of the pattern of normal classes. What are distinctive features of WSPs, you suggest, are simply matters of scale. You seem to see those matters of scale in terms of the difficulties they create for schools, whereas I see them in terms of their educational value. Although I acknowledge these difficulties, I argue that the educational values are sufficiently great to make them worth taking on, and, incidentally, while showing how the difficulties need not be as great as they might initially seem. In fact, mounting a WSP is surprisingly easy. The scale issues—the length of time, the whole school, the large product at the end—are not incidental inconveniences but are integral to the achievement of the unique educational values WSPs can deliver to the whole school community and to students' learning in particular.

Both this program and the LiD program, if thought about as investment opportunities, offer very large returns of educational value for a relatively tiny investment. Why would anyone choose not to do it? Well, of course, we are looking at the reasons, but we should try to keep our minds alert to the potential educational value, which is, after all, the purpose for which schools exist.

I suspect by "eccentric" you mean unusual. If that is a good enough reason not to try something, we are likely to see little educational improvement.

Q 10: Too massive demands made for design of WSP curriculum.

[A social studies teacher in the middle school. She is currently doing an MEd in curriculum and instruction in a nearby college.]

You keep saying that mounting a WSP is not as huge a task as it might initially seem, but I am not convinced. Much of my hesitation is due to the fact that there is no fixed or ready-made curriculum for such a project. Don't get me wrong: I am not saying that everything needs to be planned in detail, or that every teacher needs lesson plans prepared in advance for the 3 years. But I think this talk of "it's easy" underestimates how different teaching a WSP is from regular classroom activities. The fact that there is no curriculum, except what we make up on the fly, is not a problem for some teachers, but it is a very considerable problem for others. Not everyone feels comfortable taking on this kind of radically different kind of activity. I know my colleague suggests that projects are common, but, as you said, the scale of these WSPs is part of what makes them distinctive and that scale implies something most teachers will have problems adapting to. Such a project is a massive task of designing not just the topic of study, but the whole curriculum that is going to absorb so much time over 3 years.

R 10: Too massive demands made for design of WSP curriculum.

There is no denying that some teachers will feel more at home in a WSP than others. But, again, please remember that this project is not all-absorbing of students' or teachers' time. It is, however, a consistent absorber of, but also a stimulant of, intellectual energy. Once the project is under way, it becomes a topic of talk among teachers, of thought about how particular common core state standards and other curriculum objectives can also be adapted to the project, of how one's class's work can be shaped to fit the developing end product, and so on. It becomes a large and lively presence in the lives of teachers, and the school as a whole, even though it does not displace most other school activities. Rather than seeing it simply as making massive demands, it seems to me more accurate to see it as adding stimulation and energy out of proportion to the demands it makes on time and energy. In short, a WSP gives more than it takes.

One of the community-building influences of a WSP is within the teachers' group in the school. WSPs get teachers working together to plan and coordinate units and lessons. In that process, teachers share ideas and practices and much else in the way of skills and knowledge of their craft. They do this kind of thing routinely, of course—or some teachers do in some schools. But WSPs create conditions where this kind of joint planning is just a part of what happens as the project goes forward well.

One cost the school may wish to expend on the project, if possible, is funding a position for a support teacher—maybe a part-time coordinator, even a retired volunteer. Such a person can ease much of the unfamiliar aspects of the WSP. Such a person could, for example, seek out experts on the project topic who could come into the classroom to share their work and expertise with the students. If the project concerns a local geographical or historical or environmental topic, there are usually many experts and enthusiasts eager to offer their knowledge freely to schools. Indeed, there are nonprofit groups throughout the country who are waiting by the phone in hopes of offering their educational materials and, in many cases, actual programs, to schools. Many nonprofits have education specialists who will customize experiences for specific schools by request. We are not alone in our communities in our efforts to educate our children!

Again, arguments about why WSPs can't work or will be impossibly onerous are simply contradicted by those currently under way in the real world.

Q 11: Not pedagogically efficient.

[A district math specialist who has been assigned to support teachers in the primary school. He has a PhD in educational psychology and has been a co-researcher with his former supervisor on a statewide study of instructional strategies.]

Many studies have supported the fact that direct instruction gets us better results than such projects. Many of our kids also need extra help just to deal with the routine tasks in a regular classroom. This is not good pedagogy and it adds an additional inefficiency for these less able kids.

R 11: Not pedagogically efficient.

Inefficient? How do you know? WSPs are not designed to achieve some relatively short-term learning objectives, of the kind that most research studies cite to support this kind of claim. No such study has come remotely near to focusing on such a 3-year project. Also, the kinds of things WSPs teach—cooperation, pride, respect for others' abilities, and so on—are not amenable to testing by the dominant research methods currently available. Education, again, is mostly a field of values and meanings, and these are beyond the reach of the kind of research that is referred to when claims about "inefficient" learning are made.

Assertions that direct instruction is more efficient than the Project Method, such as one finds in Jeanne Chall's 2002 book, are simply misguided in a fairly crude way. These conclusions are based on studies that, at their best, study the learning outcomes on specific tasks performed by students who have been instructed according to direct instructional methods compared with those who have employed the Project Method.

But the goals of the Project Method go far beyond the attainment of certain short-term achievements on limited tests. If one of the main goals of the Project Method is the development of democratic social skills and also development of problem-solving and critical-thinking skills, where are these in the comparisons with direct instruction? Are they of insufficient educational importance to bother factoring into the studies? It seems odd to dismiss the Project Method on the basis that it is not as efficient as some other program in achieving something that is only peripheral to its main goals. WSPs, on the other hand, have deliberate academic goals, and it seems reasonable to expect quite different results from comparisons between direct instruction and WSPs, even though the same point about the different goals of the two teaching approaches needs to be borne in mind.

Q 12: Transient populations, so many kids will miss much of it. Are they learning disabled?

[Middle school counselor who also does volunteer work in the community with troubled children. She has a master's degree in counseling.]

While these kinds of projects might do well in some schools, we face a number of special difficulties that will undermine any project of the kind you describe. One of our consistent problems is the high rate of transience among our population base. And that applies also to our teacher population. You might find that, at the end of any 3-year period, there has been a 30 or 40% change over in teaching staff, and more among the student population. That high transience rate seems also to contribute to a higher than usual rate of learning disabilities among our student body. This combination of challenges would seem to make our schools not good candidates for a WSP.

R 12: Transient populations, so many kids will miss much of it. Are they learning disabled?

What is more difficult for a new student, walking in on an ongoing project in which every student can have a distinct, meaningful role, or walking in two-thirds of the way through a unit on converting fractions to decimals? The problems you identify, which will indeed impact the effectiveness of the WSP for the students who are present for only a part of it, are less of a challenge to the WSP than they are to many other areas of the curriculum. Indeed, the WSP can be supportive of such students more easily than curriculum areas where prerequisite knowledge is not in place. You would not suggest dropping math for this reason, of course. In schools we cannot plan very well for students who come or go in the middle of our programs. We can try to be flexible and help them where possible when they are with us. A WSP seems better able to deal with such problems than most of the curriculum, and might indeed alleviate problems for other curriculum areas. So, while recognizing the problem of transience, I do not see it as an adequate reason not to take on a WSP. At least, WSPs are no more of a problem for such students than most other curriculum areas.

Similarly, I think that WSPs are at least as able to support and help students with learning disabilities as is commonly managed in many areas of the curriculum. The mutual supportiveness of the WSP is such that each student can find some role to play in contributing to the developing final product. Also, what has been called the "multifaceted methodology" that the WSPs encourage should contribute to their supportiveness of less able students. Again, in my view these projects can make a contribution to ameliorating the problems you describe, and rather than using those problems as reasons to not take on a WSP their potential contribution argues rather for starting a WSP.

Q 13: You're all mad!

[The oldest member of the group, he has taught English/language arts in the middle school for more than 30 years and is eagerly looking forward to his retirement in 2 years' time. But he consistently gets the best exam results in the school.]

My daily reality is made up of tasks imposed on me that get in the way of my educating my students. These tasks seem to me to have less and less to do with education, and are less and less sensible ways of even developing the basic skills our educational masters want us to deliver. Politicians, who receive complaints about students' skills and knowledge on leaving schools, turn to whoever seems to have the loudest educational voice, or promises the results required in the simplest ways. The people who make decisions about what is done in schools are generally educationally clueless, who know nothing about the history of schools and all the things that have been tried. I've been through wave after wave of increasingly mindless programs, each of which makes cruder and cruder and narrower and narrower what we are supposed to deliver. In my time I've been asked to submit the behavioral objectives for my classes; I've had to deal with the results of some mindless voucher system some local politician forced on us—a program designed and implemented by people who knew nothing of the 19th-century British "payment by results" scheme that didn't last more than a decade or two because of the damage it caused—then I had to take workshops on recognizing students' learning styles and changing my teaching accordingly. Oh, and there was the brief period when I was guaranteed success if I could work out the structure of my subject and frame my teaching to bring that out for the students. I've been subjected to grinning idiots passing through with new and guaranteed programs to meet the latest set of district curriculum objectives; then we had the No Child Left Behind stuff, and now, even more detailed and extensive—and mindless, humorless, and dreary beyond belief—Common Core State Standards stuff. I'm also told that my problem is that I haven't been focused on evidence-based methods and haven't used scientific procedures in my literature classes. Your problem is that you are trying to promote an *educational* program. Are you out of your mind? What hope do you think it has of anyone even being able to take in what you are talking about? You are not using all the appropriate jargon of "basic skills" or "critical thinking" (though I've never been able to work out how it's supposed to be different from "thinking"). You just don't understand. The lunatics are running the asylum. And no one can make out what you are talking about when you go on about academic programs and students' understanding. You might as well be talking Latin. You have to realize, you are in the land of edu-babble, where *academic* is a dirty word and *learning* means memorizing something till the next test and *understanding* isn't a word at all because you can't give it a number. Not that I'm bitter, you understand.

R 13: You're all mad!

Right, I think I recognize a lack of bitterness when I don't hear it. Well, first, you are expressing something many people feel in education, of course. The sequence of major attempts to reform schools and teaching haven't delivered the goods with any conspicuous success, despite the huge amount of money spent, and the massive confidence of the supposed reformers. When we don't succeed, we have to find a scapegoat, and the easy scapegoat for many is teachers.

But, surely, we all face the same problem and frustration. How are we to improve education? Current rates of literacy and numeracy are just unacceptable. Students are nearly all endowed with the ability to learn to read and write and calculate with efficiency, teachers are nearly all well-trained and skillful, administrators nearly all work long hours with dedication and compassion, huge financial resources have been poured into schooling, politicians are concerned to provide what guidance they can to improve schooling—and yet, despite all this, no one can feel schools are in general doing an adequate job. And I think you are right to suggest that many of the waves of reform represent a kind of flailing at the problem.

Mind you, I have been accused of claiming that implementing a WSP isn't as hard as it may initially seem, and now you might accuse me of being a Pollyanna because I have more faith that nearly everyone in education is willing to reflect sensibly about the causes of our problems and be open to ideas about how they might be solved. The difficulty, I think, is that most people are working with too few and old ideas. Instead of trying to form or consider new ideas, they simply shuffle the old ones again. Well, that's a story for elsewhere (like Egan, 2002). Here I can only admit that there is surely something in your tirade many people recognize, but I think there are grounds to think that WSPs can find their way into many schools' practice even so. Then it will be a matter of how successful they are, by the kinds of measures we can bring to bear on them now and the studies that will follow when there are many others to research. I know, an inadequate response: I suffer from optimism.

Q 14: How many schools do you expect to see a project like these happening in?

> [The superintendent of the school district. He was a former teacher in a nearby high school and has a PhD in educational leadership from the local university.]

I'm not clear how frequently you imagine people are going to try these projects. How many schools do you imagine will do these projects? I image they might be quite rare. Do you really think a school might do one, regroup and plan for a year, and then start another? That suggests you see these as a permanent part of a school's life. Do you really think this is likely? I can think of maybe just a few schools in this region that might have the resources and interest to take on something like this.

R 14: How many schools do you expect to see a project like these happening in?

If this is a good educational idea and provides a valuable educational experience to students and teachers alike, why restrict it? I thought providing valuable educational experiences was what the school was designed to do. Why would you imagine such an experience as appropriate in only rare conditions? Even if it takes some effort to launch the first WSP in a school, it will be found that this novel program and experience can quite easily become part of the everyday routine of schools. The main obstacle to launching a WSP is not its educational value, clearly, but rather the fact that it is something new and unfamiliar, and it requires an act of imagination to see how it can be brought into everyday reality, and it requires a bit of work. That it might be an administrative challenge is not a sufficient reason to fail to take on the challenge: We do not want to have the administrative tail wag the educational dog. Now I am no doubt being excessively defensive here, imagining reluctance to give a good educational idea a try in our schools because it requires forms of planning and implementation that are unfamiliar. Experience suggests— as with the Learning in Depth program—that once begun the return to teachers and students in educational benefits, and also job-satisfaction benefits, and community-enriching benefits, far outweigh initial fears about the unfamiliar work of getting it going. I see no reason why WSPs do not become a normal part of normal schools' normal functioning. So, how many schools? As with the Learning in Depth program—all.

CONCLUSION

If you have read this far—unless you are being compelled to read the book for a course or for a review—I hope that you think it is worthwhile to put the WSP idea into wider practice. (And even if you are reading it under compulsion of some sort, I hope you will have reached the same conclusion.) One problem with facing a new kind of program is that most schools are over-bursting with programs and activities, and simply covering the mandated curriculum is a challenge many can't adequately meet. The school, as it currently exists, is a place full of generally stressed workers on whose shoulders society seems intent on piling more and more to be done—not all of it of notable educational value. The view from the regular classroom is one constricted by the range of requirements in place that take all the time available, and then some. What chance for WSPs in such a context?

I don't know. But I have this slightly bizarre faith that if some innovation promises to deliver significant educational benefits at the cost of some, but far from overwhelming, administrative inconvenience and some disruption of regular scheduling, then everyone should set about giving it a try. But the equation is actually even more strongly in favor of giving it a try, in that it isn't just a matter of weighing some intangible educational benefit against administrative inconvenience, but also one needs to add to the "give it a try" side the rewards to students, teachers, and administrators of working together as an energized learning community. One needs to add the further difficult-to-weigh but very tangible benefits of invigorated learning, enthusiastic students, and teachers also engaged in learning about a new topic along with the whole school community.

What is to stop WSPs becoming a regular part of the schooling experience of students? There is a library of books about educational change, obstacles to change, and what we need to do to bring about change (e.g., Fullan, 2011a, 2011b; Goodson, 2005, 2013; Hargreaves, 2003; Hargreaves & Fullan, 2012; Hargreaves & Shirley, 2012). If you are persuaded that WSPs represent a good educational idea, and that the arguments I have made for how they might be brought into reality are plausible, then the next step is up to you.

References

21st Century Schools. (2014, April). Available at www.21stcenturyschools. com/What_is_21st_Century_Education.htm

Barkley, E. F., Cross, K. P., & Major, C. H. (2005). *Collaborative learning techniques*. San Francisco, CA: Wiley.

Barone, T. E., & Eisner, E.W. (2011). *Arts based research*. Thousand Oaks, CA: Sage.

Bettelheim, B. (1976). *The uses of enchantment*. New York, NY: Knopf.

Bolak, K., Bialach, D., & Duhnphy, M. (2005). Standards-based, thematic units integrate the arts and energize students and teachers. *Middle School Journal, 31*(2), 57–60.

Bruner, J. (1988). Discussion. *Yale Journal of Criticism. 2*(1), 28–37.

Chall, J. (2002). *The Academic Achievement Challenge: What really works in the classroom?* New York, NY: The Guilford Press.

Collins, A., Brown, J. S., & Newman, S. E. (1989). Cognitive apprenticeship: Teaching the crafts of reading, writing, and mathematics. In L. B. Resnick (Ed.), *Knowing, learning, and instruction: Essays in honor of Robert Glaser* (pp. 453–494). Hillsdale, NJ: Lawrence Erlbaum Associates.

Comer, J. P., & Haynes, N. M. (1992, June). *Summary of school development program effects*. New Haven, CT: Yale Child Study Center.

Cronbach, L., & Snow, R. (1977). *Aptitudes and instructional methods: A handbook for research on interactions*. New York, NY: Irvington.

Cullingford, C. (1991). *The inner world of the school*. London, UK: Cassell.

Davis, B. G. (1993). *Tools for teaching*. San Francisco, CA: Jossey-Bass.

Egan, K. (1997). *The educated mind: How cognitive tools shape our understanding*. Chicago, IL: University of Chicago Press.

Egan, K. (2002). *Getting it wrong from the beginning: Our progressivist inheritance from Herbert Spencer, John Dewey, and Jean Piaget*. New Haven, CT: Yale University Press.

Egan, K. (2005). *An imaginative approach to teaching*. San Francisco, CA: Jossey-Bass.

Egan, K. (2008). *The future of education: Reimagining our schools from the ground up*. New Haven, CT: Yale University Press.

Egan, K. (2011). *Learning in depth: A simple innovation that can transform schooling.* Chicago, IL: University of Chicago Press.

Egan, K., Cant, A., & Judson, G. (Eds.). (2013). *Wonder-full education: The centrality of wonder in teaching and learning across the curriculum.* New York, NY: Routledge.

Eisner, E. W. (2001). *The educational imagination.* (3rd ed.). Englewood Cliffs, NJ: Prentice Hall.

Epstein, J. L. (1995, May). School-family-community partnerships: Caring for the children we share. *Phi Delta Kappan, 76*(9), 701–712.

Fisher, B. (1995). *Thinking and learning together: Curriculum and community in a primary classroom.* Portsmouth, NH: Heinemann.

Fitzpatrick, J. L., Sanders, J. R., & Worthen, B. R. (2010). *Program evaluation: Alternative approaches and practical guidelines* (4th ed.). Englewood Cliffs, NJ: Prentice Hall.

Flowers, N., Mertens, S. B., & Mulhall, P. F. (1999). The impact of teaming: Five research-based outcomes. *Middle School Journal, 36*(5), 9–19.

Fullan, M. (2004). *Leadership and sustainability: Systems thinkers in action.* Thousand Oaks, CA: Corwin Press.

Fullan, M. (2011a). *Change leader: Learning to do what matters most.* San Francisco, CA: Jossey-Bass.

Fullan, M. (2011b). *The six secrets of change: What the best leaders do to help their organizations survive and thrive.* San Francisco, CA: Jossey-Bass.

Gardner, H. (1983). *Frames of mind: The theory of multiple intelligences.* New York, NY: Basic Books.

Gardner, H. (1993). *The unschooled mind: How children think and how schools should teach.* New York, NY: Basic Books.

Gardner, H. (2006). *Multiple intelligences: New horizons in theory and practice.* New York, NY: Basic Books.

Gardner, H. (2009). *Five minds for the future.* Cambridge, MA: Harvard Business School Press.

Gardner H., & Winner, E. (1979). The development of metaphoric competence: Implications for humanistic disciplines. In S. Sacks, (Ed.). *On metaphor* (pp. 121–139). Chicago, IL: University of Chicago Press.

Goddard, Y. L., Goddard, R. D., & Tschannen-Moran, M. (2007). A theoretical and empirical investigation of teacher collaboration for school improvement and student achievement in public elementary schools. *Teachers College Record, 109*(4), 877–896.

Goodlad, J. (2004) *A place called school* (20th Anniversary Edition). New York, NY: McGraw-Hill.

Goodson, I. (2005). *Learning, curriculum and life politics: The selected works of Ivor F. Goodson.* London, UK: Routledge.

Goodson, I. (2013). *School subjects and curriculum change.* London, UK: Routledge.

Grant, K.B., & Ray, J. A. (2009). *Home, school, and community collaboration: Culturally responsive family involvement.* Thousand Oaks, CA: Sage.

Gutek, G. L. (1978). *Joseph Neef: The Americanization of Pestalozzianism.* Tuscaloosa, AL: University of Alabama Press.

Hallinger, P., & Heck, H. (2009). Distributed leadership in schools: Does system policy make a difference? *Studies in Educational Leadership,* (7), Part II, 101–117.

Hargreaves, A. (2003). *Teaching in the knowledge society: Education in the age of insecurity.* New York, NY: Teachers College Press.

Hargreaves, A., & Fullan, M. (2012). *Professional capital: Transforming teaching in every school.* New York, NY: Teachers College Press.

Hargreaves, A., & Shirley, D. L. (2012). *The global fourth way: The quest for educational excellence.* Thousand Oaks, CA: Corwin Press.

Havelock, E. A. (1963). *Preface to Plato.* Cambridge, MA: Harvard University Press.

Havelock, E. A. (1986). *The muse learns to write.* New Haven, CT: Yale University Press.

Henderson, A. T., & Berla, N. (Eds.) (1994). *A new generation of evidence: The family is critical to student achievement.* Washington, DC: National Committee for Citizens in Education.

Hirst, P. (1974). *Knowledge and the curriculum.* London, UK: Routledge and Kegan Paul.

Innis, H. (1951). *The bias of communication.* Toronto, Canada: University of Toronto Press.

Jackson, P. W. (1990). *Life in classrooms.* New York, NY: Teachers College Press.

Judson, G. (2010). *A new approach to ecological education: Engaging students' imaginations in their world.* New York, NY: Lang.

Judson, G. (2014). *Engaging imagination in ecological education: A practical guide for teachers.* Vancouver, BC: Pacific Educational Press.

Katz, L., & Chard, S. (2000). *Engaging children's minds* (2nd. ed.). New York, NY: Praeger.

Kermode, F. (1966). *The sense of an ending.* Oxford, UK: Oxford University Press.

Kilpatrick, W. H. (1918). The project method. *Teachers College Record, 19*(4), 319–335.

Knoll, M. (1997). The project method: Its vocational education origin and international development. *Journal of Industrial Teacher Education, 34*(3), 59–80.

Lévi-Strauss, C. (1966). *The savage mind*. Chicago, IL: University of Chicago Press.

Lortie, D. C. (2002). *Schoolteacher: A sociological study* (2nd ed.). Chicago, IL: University of Chicago Press.

McClure, C. T. (2008). The benefits of teacher collaboration. *District Administration*, Sept. Available at www.districtadministration.com/article/benefits-teacher-collaboration/

Michaelsen, L. K., Knight, A. B., & Fink, L. D. (Eds.). (2002). *Team based learning: A transformative use of small groups*. Sterling, VA: Stylus Publishing.

Miller, P. (2010). *Smart swarm*. London, UK: Collins.

Murphy, P. (1995). *Comenius: A reassessment of his life and work*. Dublin, Ireland: Irish Academic Press.

Noddings, N. (2005). *The challenge to care in schools: An alternative approach to education* (2nd ed.). New York, NY: Teachers College Press.

Ong, W. (1982). *Orality and literacy*. London and New York: Methuen.

Pashler, H., McDaniel, M., Rohrer, D., & Bjork, R. (2009). Learning styles: Concepts and evidence. *Psychological Science in the Public Interest, 9*,105–119.

Pask, G. (1976). Styles and strategies of learning. *British Journal of Educational Psychology,46*(2), 128–148.

Postman, N., & Weingartner, C. (1969). *Teaching as a subversive activity*. New York, NY: Delacorte Press.

Putnam, R. D. (2000). *Bowling alone. The collapse and revival of American community*. New York, NY: Simon & Schuster.

Putnam, R. D. (Ed.). (2002). *Democracies in flux: The evolution of social capital in contemporary society*. New York, NY: Oxford University Press.

Resnick, L. (Ed.). (1989). *Knowing, learning, and instruction*. Hillsdale, NJ: Lawrence Erlbaum Associates.

Sanders, J. R., & Sullins, C. D. (Eds.). (2005). *Evaluating school programs: An educator's guide*. Thousand Oaks, CA: Corwin Press.

Seeley, T. D. (2010). *Honeybee democracy*. Princeton, NJ: Princeton University Press.

Sergiovanni, T. (1994). *Building community in schools*. San Francisco, CA: Jossey-Bass.

Spencer, H. (1966). *Education: Intellectual, moral, and physical*. (Vol. XVI of the Works of Herbert Spencer). Osnabrük, Germany: Zeller. (Original work published 1854–1859)

Stahl, S. A. (2002). Different strokes for different folks? In L. Abbeduto (Ed.), *Taking sides: Clashing on controversial issues in educational psychology* (pp. 98–107). Guilford, CT: McGraw-Hill.

Stufflebeam, D., Madaus, G., & Kelleghan, T. (Eds.). (2000). *Evaluation models: Viewpoints on educational and human services evaluation*. Boston, MA: Kluwer.

Thousand, J. S., Villa, R. A., & Nevin, A. I. (2006). The many faces of collaborative planning and teaching. *Theory Into Practice, 45*(3), 239–248.

Tomlinson, C. A. (2004). *How to differentiate instruction in mixed ability classrooms* (2nd ed.). Alexandria, VA: ASCD.

Vygotsky, L. (1962). *Thought and language* (Eugenia Haufmann & Gertrude Vakar, Trans.). Cambridge, MA: MIT Press.

Vygotsky, L. S. (1978). *Mind in society: The development of higher psychological processes*. Cambridge, MA: Harvard University Press.

Index

175

About the Author and Contributors

Kieran Egan is a professor of education at Simon Fraser University, Burnaby, British Columbia. He is a recipient of the Grawemeyer Award in Education and an Upton Sinclair Award, is an AERA Fellow, National Academy of Education member, a Fellow of the Royal Society of Canada, a Canada Research Chair in Education, among other awards and prizes. He is the author of many books, including the best-selling *The Educated Mind: How Cognitive Tools Shape our Understanding* and *The Future of Education: Reimagining Our Schools from the Ground up*.

Bob Dunton is the director and co-founder of Corbett Charter School in Corbett, Oregon, USA. He has worked in public education as a teacher and administrator for 24 years. Bob's teaching experience includes 8 years working in villages up and down the Alaska Peninsula and his administrative experience spans 12 years as superintendent of two Oregon school districts. He has been an engaged advocate for Imaginative Education in venues as diverse as the Confederation of Oregon School Administrators, the National Charter Schools Conference, and regional and national Advanced Placement conferences, but his passion remains his work with teachers and students. Bob is interested in educational theory, school design, and curriculum and instruction.

Gillian Judson is a lecturer at Simon Fraser University in British Columbia, Canada, and one of the directors of the Imaginative Education Research Group (IERG). She is author of the books *Engaging Imagination in Ecological Education: Implementing A Meaningful Approach* (Pacific Educational Press, 2014) and *A New Approach to Ecological Education: Engaging Students' Imaginations in Their World* (Peter Lang, 2010), and co-editor of the book *Wonder-full Education: The Centrality of Wonder in Teaching and Learning Across the Curriculum* (Routledge, 2013). Her research is primarily concerned with sustainability and how an ecologically sensitive and imaginative approach to education can both increase students' engagement with, and understanding of, the usual content of the curriculum but how showing it in a light can lead to a sophisticated ecological consciousness. Her research interests also include teacher education, professional development, and social studies education.